RETHINKING THE WAR ON DRUGS IN IRELAND

UNDERCURRENTS

Published titles in the series

UNDERCURRENTS Series Editor Fintan O'Toole

Rethinking the War on Drugs in Ireland

TIM MURPHY

CORK
UNIVERSITY
PRESS

First published in 1996 by
Cork University Press
University College
Cork
Ireland

British Library Cataloguing in Publication Data

A CIP catalogue record for this book is available from the British Library

ISBN 1 85918 070 1

Typeset in Ireland by Seton Music Graphics Ltd, Co. Cork
Printed in Ireland by ColourBooks, Baldoyle, Co. Dublin

CONTENTS

ACKNOWLEDGEMENTS

I would like to thank all those people – family, friends and colleagues – who encouraged and assisted me in the course of writing this pamphlet. I am particularly grateful to the following for their valuable comments on early drafts: Shashikala Gurpura, Anne Murphy, Gerard Staunton, and Professors Paul O'Higgins, David Gwynn Morgan and Garrett Barden. Responsibility for any errors or faults in the text is mine.

Special thanks to Ger, and to Shashi.

Tim Murphy
August 1996

1. INTRODUCTION

This pamphlet presents an argument for the legalization of the psychoactive drugs that are currently prohibited by law. To many, this suggestion will seem preposterous and irresponsible. The most common representations of drugs, those emanating from the political sphere and the various organs of the media, are almost uniformly opposed to such an idea. Drugs are described as a 'scourge' or 'menace' that threaten the essence of our social order. The elements that comprise this monolithic threat include the following: drugs are regarded, in part because of a definitive addictive quality, as dangerous to the individual and harmful to families and society in general; drug use is considered to be unacceptable and morally wrong; and drugs are thought to be the central reason underlying increases in the crime rate and the growth of organized, vicious-minded, criminal gangs. In the light of these perspectives, the 'war on drugs' is regarded as self-evidently necessary and correct, and the notion of legalization appears as a form of surrender to terrorist forces.

The extent to which these views are supported in the public domain – and my impression is that this support constitutes a majority – is a measure of an extremely important ideological triumph for those who hold political and economic power within the state. This support signals the prevalence of a set of ideas about drugs that have never been subjected to a thorough *analysis*. It is nothing short of incredible that this important area of public policy, while the subject of a great deal of rhetoric, has not been properly examined or reviewed. Instead, the tendency of political figures and the media is towards simplification and, even more significantly, conflation: drugs, drug use, drug abuse, drug dealing, drug criminals – all of these merge to become a threatening entity ('drugs') against which we have no choice but to wage war. Further, 'drugs' are often seen in isolation from, and given priority over, other social questions: despite high levels of unemployment, poverty, and emigration, they appear to be justified as a consuming political passion.

Drugs and drug use are extraordinarily complex phenomena. Aldous Huxley described the story of drug-taking as 'one of the most curious and . . . most significant chapters in the natural history of human beings'.[1] The personal and the political are simultaneously implicated in drug use, and the implications are unique and intricate. By exploring some of this complexity, this pamphlet attempts to redress the balance in the public representations of drugs and drug use. When the issues are confronted in a rational manner, I believe that present drug policy and drug laws are exposed as misguided and unjust.

There are basically two ideal-typical perspectives on drug policy.[2] The first – the 'deterrence' perspective – is based, in my view, on denial: it is the belief that the best way to prevent the problems arising from the use of drugs is to try to eliminate their use altogether. On the other hand, the second perspective – the 'normalization' perspective – is founded on acknowledgement: in this view, the problems arising from the use of drugs are not inevitable, and are intensified rather than alleviated by attempts to eliminate their use.

The deterrence perspective provides the rationale for the ongoing 'war on drugs' which is fought by governments in Ireland and elsewhere, and also for the prohibitionist legal arrangements associated with that 'war'. This perspective is historically linked to a strategy of intervention in dealing with social problems based on differentiation and exclusion. It is associated with a positivist world-view, adhering to the belief that human beings are essentially responsive organisms, acted upon by external forces. In this perspective, 'drug problems' are caused primarily by the substances themselves and, only in a determined sense, by the individuals who ingest them. The 'models' of drug use that are contained within the parameters of this perspective include the 'medical' model – warning that these substances are dependence-producing and that such dependence constitutes a 'disease' – and the 'moral-legal' model – condemning all illicit drugs as dangerous and all illicit drug use as wrong. The main Irish drug policy document, the 1991 *Government Strategy to Prevent Drug Misuse*,[3] is clearly situated within this 'deterrence' perspective. The report advocates the four typical 'strategy measures' designed to combat 'drug misuse'. Of these, three are oriented primarily towards the war on drugs: 'supply reduction' (the use of criminal sanctions to deter the distribution and sale of illicit drugs); 'demand reduction' (preventive measures, including preventive forms of drug education, to discourage the use of illicit drugs); and 'international co-operation' (supply-reduction measures at the level of the European Union and other international organizations).

The war on drugs, however, is not a total war. The other strategy measure in the 1991 report is 'education and manpower training'. This involves measures, including treatment services, directed towards reducing the harm caused by drug misuse. 'Harm reduction', which is given a secondary role in the war on drugs (and usually only at the treatment level), belongs more to the 'normalization' perspective on drug policy. This perspective is linked to integrative or 'normalizing', rather than exclusionary, strategies of social policy. It is founded on a world-view associated with interpretative and transactional epistemologies. These knowledge systems regard the individual as an agent acting meaningfully in given social contexts, contexts which in turn have the potential to construct meanings of various kinds. In the context of drug use, the individual and the social circumstances of drug use are regarded as more significant than the physiological possibilities of any chemical agent.

The first of the two models of drug use in the normalization perspective is the 'psychosocial' model: drug use is regarded as behaviour that would not persist unless it serves some meaningful function for the individual user in a given social context. The second model – the 'sociocultural' model – incorporates the variable social and psychological considerations of the previous model but goes further to highlight socioeconomic and environmental conditions as the reasons for psychological demands and stresses of various kinds.

If drug policy is to be seriously concerned with limiting the problems that drug use can cause, I propose that it should be based not on the positivist deterrence perspective with its moral-legal and medical models of drug use, but rather on the interpretative normalization perspective and, in particular, on sociocultural models of drug use. Contrary to the belief that drugs themselves are the cause of drug problems, I will argue that the war on drugs intensifies the problems associated with drug use and also has other negative and costly effects. Drug policy, therefore, should be guided mainly by a version of the normalization philosophy of harm reduction. In accordance with this version, drug laws should be changed from the present prohibitionist arrangements to a form of regulation that would rely to a far lesser extent on the criminal sanction.[4] Although such reform is referred to as 'legalization', it should be emphasized that the question is not whether criminal law should play a role in this area, but rather how such a criminal law should be constructed. The criminal law, after all, has a potential role in most human activity; it represents a line that could be transgressed at any given moment. The sale of alcohol to *minors*, for example, is an offence.[5] Therefore, just as with licit drugs now, the 'legalization' of other drugs would include restrictions and conditions on the distribution and sale of drugs relating to, for example, age, and time and place of sale; in addition, different restrictions and conditions would apply to different drugs.

Legalization is not offered as the 'solution' to the problems associated with drugs. There are two main reasons for this. Firstly, legal forms, very noticeably, have 'a logic that is in tension with the social realities to which [they are] applied'.[6] In the present context, this 'tension' means that while various drugs, in certain circumstances, have the potential to kill or injure seriously the individuals who consume them, the law is incapable of completely controlling this possibility. (This is not in any way to belittle the harm which drugs, both licit and illicit, can cause. As this pamphlet will demonstrate, the motivation behind the integrative normalization perspective on drug use is precisely the greatest possible reduction of the harm caused by drugs.)

Secondly, drug use and drug law do not exist in a social vacuum. The proposal that policy should be guided by normalization understandings of drug use requires a switch in perception away from the current deterrence emphasis on the centrality and 'dangers' of the illicit substances themselves to an acknowledgement that drugs only ever represent one element in complex human and social processes. Drug misuse can never be understood – let alone regulated in a relatively controlled and safe manner – in isolation from diverse environmental influences. The insights which accompany the normalization perspective, as I interpret them, require that drug legalization be initiated in the context of a multisectoral response on the part of the state. While it is my contention that the problems associated with drugs can be reduced significantly by means of legalization, I will also argue that other social reform and restructuring is required for drug problems to be tackled in the most effective way possible.

The next chapter places present drug laws in historical perspective. This involves tracing the rise of the deterrence perspective as the base for drug policy during the nineteenth and early twentieth centuries. This chapter will discuss the different historical roles of the medical and moral-legal models of drug use in shaping the drug policies of Britain and the United States. It will also outline briefly the influence of the two models on Irish drug policy.

The third chapter introduces the concepts of 'drug', 'set' and 'setting'. 'Set' and 'setting' are references to the individual and social circumstances of drug use, circumstances which in turn determine the nature, extent, and potential consequences of the drug use. These interpretative concepts, and not the 'drug', are the critical factors in drug use. This chapter applies 'set' and 'setting' to the construct of 'drug addiction' and demonstrates that the medical model of drug use, which is founded on an absolutist notion of dependence, is fundamentally flawed as a basis for drug policy. This chapter concludes by introducing some behavioural interpretations of drug use and misuse, particularly those related to socioeconomic deprivation.

The fourth chapter addresses the moral aspects of drug use and the related question of the proper scope of the criminal law. It is often argued that the criminalization of drug-related activity is justified on 'moral' grounds. Arguments of this kind display a basic disregard for the psychosocial and sociocultural understandings of drug use and problematic drug use. This chapter questions the legitimacy of present drug controls by situating the moral condemnation of drugs and drug users within the moral, political, and economic context of contemporary Western culture.

The fifth chapter bolsters the argument by examining the effects and the costs of prohibition as it operates in Ireland. Prohibition is not only shown to be seriously failing to meet its objectives, it is also shown to be creating much of what is generally regarded as the 'drug problem'. This chapter will argue that present policy is both ineffectual and irresponsible.

The sixth chapter discusses some aspects of the legalization policy option, including some typical objections. While not presenting a detailed blueprint of any kind, this chapter is based on the premise, established by the preceding chapters, that a complete block regarding the idea of legalization is not justified.

2. DRUG PROHIBITION IN
HISTORICAL PERSPECTIVE

A drug may be broadly defined as 'a chemical which causes changes in the way the human body functions, either mentally, physically, or emotionally'.[7] Of those drugs which are now used in a non-medical context, some are natural, such as alcohol and opium; others are synthetic, such as lysergic acid diethylamide (LSD or 'acid') and methylene dioxy metaamphetamine (MDMA or 'Ecstasy'); others still, such as heroin and cocaine, are artificial forms of naturally occurring substances. Typically (albeit to very different degrees), these drugs interfere with cell functions either by depressing or stimulating the central nervous system, or by inducing hallucinations, or some combination of these. Some basic information concerning the most popular drugs which are presently used in the non-medical context is contained in the Appendix.

There are basically three forms of legal control over drugs used in this way. Alcohol and nicotine, for example, are drugs which are integral and 'acceptable' elements of contemporary Western cultures and, as such, legal restrictions on their availability are typically minimal. Other drugs which are sometimes used for non-medical purposes, like barbiturates and benzodiazepines, also have legitimate medical uses. These drugs are only available on the basis of medical prescription. The final legal control is usually referred to as 'prohibition'. As provided in Ireland by the Misuse of Drugs Act 1977, it is normally a criminal offence to manufacture, distribute, sell, or possess any of the drugs in this category.[8] The 'criminalized' drugs are the same in most Western states; the most widely used are cannabis, amphetamine, MDMA, LSD, heroin, and cocaine.

The genesis of drug prohibition and of contemporary deterrence drug policies generally is to be found in changing perceptions of the use of two drugs – alcohol and opium – during the nineteenth century. It was, in fact, perceptions of the use of alcohol which originally precipitated the development of legal controls; only much later were perceptions of the use of opium to contribute to this process. This chapter contains a brief historical account of drug-policy developments in the United Kingdom and the United States during the late nineteenth and early twentieth centuries, and concludes with a discussion of the more recent Irish drug-policy choices in the light of these historical developments.[9]

In Britain, the eighteenth century was 'an era of prodigious drinking of alcohol'.[10] The drug was regarded as safe and a regular supply was believed to be essential to good health; these perceptions, coupled with the vital social function served by the tavern, meant that alcohol was even 'accorded a very high esteem'.[11] Although drunkenness was, generally speaking, punishable, it was not the target of severe moral condemnation. Further, and very significantly, it was believed that there was 'nothing . . . to explain, only to correct'.[12] During the nineteenth century, however, 'alcoholism' emerged as a 'social problem'. As to the reasons for this development, Nick Heather and Ian Robertson note that 'Precisely why the [nineteenth] century discovered a major social problem where none existed before is mysterious. It cannot have been due to any increase in the amount consumed because no such increase occurred.'[13]

There were, it would seem, a variety of contributory factors. The dramatic changes wrought by the Industrial Revolution were certainly pivotal in the construction of this 'social problem'.[14] Thus, one account places emphasis on the fact that drinking became a threat to the factory-based economic substructure of the new order; in addition,

> the great increase in economic and social mobility and
> the emergence of bewildering changes in moral values

> which accompanied the break-up of the old order
> seemed to fragment networks of deference and respect
> and threaten to swamp existing institutions of social
> control . . . drunkenness caused anxiety to conser-
> vative interests because it appeared to be a precursor of
> social chaos.[15]

Another, related, aspect of the transformation is highlighted by Peter Gay's examination of the 'advice literature' of the nineteenth century – a literature written by, and on behalf of, a bourgeoisie 'anxious . . . over whether they could manage a world apparently spinning out of control'.[16] The literature reveals an obsession with self-control and temperance which was unleashed on a hitherto largely unsuspecting world.[17] 'The nineteenth-century bourgeoisie', Gay proclaims flatly, 'did have its own recognizable preferred neurotic style, and that style was obsessional-compulsive neurosis'.[18] Ultimately, alcoholism became a social problem due to 'medical imperialism' – 'the tendency of sections of the medical profession to claim increasingly diverse types of human problems as their own special areas of expertise'.[19] Certain private conduct, including excessive drinking, that formerly might have been regarded as 'sinful', gradually became a subject of medical science.

The medical model of drug use is based on the idea that 'drug addiction' constitutes a 'disease'. This notion originated with the highly influential Temperance Movement, which campaigned against alcohol consumption throughout the nineteenth and early twentieth centuries. The seeds of this movement had actually been sown in the late eighteenth century by two men on different sides of the Atlantic: Benjamin Rush in the United States and Thomas Trotter in Britain. In 1785, Rush, one of the foremost medical practitioners of his time, published his famous work, *An Inquiry into the Effects of Ardent Spirits upon the Human Body and Mind with an Account of the Means of Preventing and of the Remedies for Curing Them.* Trotter's equivalent publication was, in 1804, *An Essay, Medical, Philosophical and Chemical on Drunkenness*. Rush and Trotter simultaneously laid the foundation for the disease theory of alcohol addiction – the idea that alcohol was an addictive substance and that addiction was a 'disease of the will' (Rush) or a 'disease of the mind' (Trotter). Their basic understanding was that, once addicted, the addict was powerless to resist 'cravings' for alcohol. The only possible successful treatment, according to Rush and Trotter, was total abstinence. (In fact, in Rush's theory, this meant total abstinence only from 'ardent spirits' and not fermented alcoholic drinks like beer and wine).[20] The disease theory of alcoholism was a classic example of nineteenth-century positivism – the application of the methods and principles of natural science to the explanation of human behaviour:

> It is perhaps difficult now to realise just how revolutionary this proposal was at the time. In the classical view of human nature. . . . the idea that human behaviour was determined by forces outside the individual's control and that it was susceptible to natural, scientific explanations would have been greeted with astonishment by the majority of people; it was implicitly assumed that men always acted freely in accordance with rational principles of self-interest. . . . The notion that people behaved the way they did, not because they wanted to, but because they could not choose otherwise would have been simply incomprehensible.[21]

The changed perceptions of alcohol use, in turn, were applied to opium use, and the same disease theory was invoked. The widespread availability and use of opiates in nineteenth-century Britain can be appreciated 'when one recalls that opium was one of the very few available effective drugs for the treatment of pain and such common ailments as fevers, diarrhoea, influenza, colds, bronchitis, and so on. In its popularity it may be likened to present-day use of drugs such as aspirin.'[22] Similarly, in the United States, it was a time when 'anyone could go to his corner druggist and buy grams of morphine or heroin for just a few pennies'.[23] Addiction to opium, as with alcohol addiction previously, was regarded as a mere 'bad habit', or, as another writer has put it, 'the excess of normal indulgence'.[24] The reactions to the 1821 publication of Thomas De Quincey's *Confessions of an English Opium Eater* have been described as follows: 'Extensive medical discussions of the habit as revealed by De Quincey were notably absent. . . . The subject could even be a matter for humour, and comment focused in the main on the literary merits of the book, the identity of the anonymous "opium-eater" and whether his account was fact or fiction.'[25]

It was 'commercial morality' which guided nineteenth-century opium policy.[26] The two 'Opium Wars' (1840–1842 and 1856), for example, were waged by British imperial forces against China to ensure that the smuggling of opium into China by the British East India Company was unimpeded by the Chinese authorities.[27] Certainly, increasing numbers of cases of opium poisoning were an influential factor in bringing about the initial regulation of opium in the British Pharmacy Act of 1868, but more significant still was the emerging professionalization of chemists and druggists. The general control in the 1868 legislation limited sales of certain drugs to pharmacists and ended sales in other shops. The specific controls were not very restrictive. For example, opium was only required to be sold in a properly labelled container. Further, many patent medicines that included opium were excluded from the legislation.[28] Essentially, its effect was to ensure a monopoly for the pharmacists in the sale and supply of drugs. 'Potential harm from drugs and poisons was the overt issue, but the benefit to pharmacists was a commercial one.'[29]

The major impetus behind the development of the disease theory of opium addiction was the increased medical use of hypodermic morphine after the invention of the hypodermic needle during the

1850s. Unlike opium, hypodermic morphine was usually administered medically; any problems in its use were thus closely linked to
the medical profession.[30] As Gerry Stimson and Edna Oppenheimer
put it, 'What emerged from the debate about the growing problem
of "morphinomania" was a construction of habitual drug use as a
disease.'[31] At the same time, although 'the theoretical foundation,
scope, and direction' of the laws which were enacted as a consequence of these developments 'were provided primarily by the
scientific conclusions earlier reached by physicians and psychiatrists',[32] the 'scientific' aspect of the disease theory of addiction
should not be overestimated. During the nineteenth century, this
was rarely, if ever, a purely medical theory. Instead, it normally
comprised two elements: the medical *and* the moral. 'The earlier
"moral tolerance" of the condition [i.e. addiction] as a bad habit
was replaced by a more severe moral as well as medical condemnation. . . . Addiction was disease *and* vice: it was "moral
bankruptcy", "disease of the will", "a form of mental insanity".'[33]
Certainly, the emphasis given to the two elements was variable:
whereas the 'vice' or moral-legal approach tended more towards
the advocacy of penal sanctions to 'punish' addicts, the expanding
medical profession placed more emphasis on the idea of disease
itself, viewing it more as an organic problem rather than as a failure
of self-control. In terms of treatment recommendations, the vice
perspective tended to advocate harsh measures, including abrupt
withdrawal, while the desired treatments from the medical point of
view were gradual withdrawal or maintenance on low dosages of
opiates.[34]

In the United States, policy towards cocaine and the opiates, as
well as towards alcohol, was radically and definitively transformed
into the punitive moral-legal approach in the first twenty years of
this century.[35] The 'moral perfectionism' of various religious forces
was instrumental in bringing about the eighteenth amendment to
the Constitution; enacted in 1919, this made it a federal crime to

possess alcohol even for drinking within the home.[36] As for cocaine and the opiates, their legislative history in the United States is tied up with racial prejudice: 'The movement to limit access to opium and its derivatives appears to have been precipitated not by a concern for the addictive properties of the drug . . . but by anti-Chinese sentiment.'[37] In an 1886 decision, for example, the Oregon district court acknowledged that 'Smoking opium is not our vice, and therefore it may be that this legislation proceeds more from a desire to vex and annoy the "Heathen Chinee" in this respect, than to protect the people from the evil habit.'[38]

The federal government enacted the Harrison Narcotic Act in 1914.[39] In fact, this legislation was essentially a taxing measure: designed to force disclosure and compliance with rules of cocaine and opium distribution and thereby eliminate competition posed to 'legitimate' physicians and pharmacists, it established a straight-forward prescription system and thereby provided for professional self-regulation.[40] 'It is unlikely that a single legislator realized in 1914 that the law Congress was passing would later be deemed a prohibition law.'[41]

In the landmark 1919 Supreme Court decision in *Webb* v. *United States*,[42] however, the regulatory 1914 Act was given a prohibitionist interpretation. Law-enforcement authorities succeeded in arguing that addiction was not a 'disease' and that the addict who seeks a 'maintenance dose' was therefore not supplied, as the legislation provided, 'in the course of [a doctor's] professional practice'. The prescription of controlled drugs to addicts was thus prohibited. The image of addiction as an 'immoral vice' – which law enforcement authorities had used to defeat the disease theory – fulfilled itself: clinics that had opened were all shut by 1923, crime by addicts increased dramatically, and many physicians who continued to pre-scribe were also arrested.[43] In 1930, a separate Bureau of Narcotics was established in the Treasury Department, and as Richard Bonnie and Charles Whitebread have observed, 'The existence of this separate bureau having responsibility . . . for narcotics enforcement . . . inevitably led to a particularly prosecutorial view of the narcotics addict'.[44] The bureau was also instrumental, allegedly in conjunction with vested corporate interests, in the later introduction of nationwide marijuana prohibition in 1937.[45] Although the phrase 'war on drugs' was not coined until 1969 by Richard Nixon,[46] this had been the philosophy underlying drug policy in the United States since the 1920s.

In Britain, on the other hand, and despite some significant movement towards the moral-legal model during and in the immediate aftermath of the First World War,[47] the 1926 report of the Departmental Committee on Morphine and Heroin Addiction (known, after its chairman, as 'the Rolleston report') emphasized the 'organic' aspect of the disease theory and thereby caused it to be regarded, initially at least, more as a medical matter:

> There was general agreement that in most well-established cases the condition must be regarded as a manifestation of disease and not as a mere form of vicious indulgence. In other words, the drug is taken in such cases not for the purposes of obtaining positive pleasure, but in order to relieve a morbid and over-powering craving. The actual need for the drug in extreme cases is in fact so great that, if it be not administered, great physical distress, culminating in actual collapse and even death, may result, unless special precautions are taken such as can only be carried out under close medical supervision, and with careful nursing.[48]

The committee concluded that the prescription of heroin and morphine to certain addicts could be regarded as 'legitimate medical treatment' under certain conditions and for certain classes of patients. The first class included those patients who were undergoing treatment 'for the cure of addiction by the gradual withdrawal method'.[49] The second class included

> persons for whom, after every effort has been made for the cure of addiction, the drug cannot be completely withdrawn either because: (i) Complete withdrawal produces serious symptoms which cannot be satisfactorily treated under the ordinary conditions of private practice; or (ii) The patient, while capable of leading a useful and fairly normal life so long as he takes a certain non-progressive quantity, usually small, of the drug of addiction, ceases to be able to do so when the regular allowance is withdrawn.[50]

The report of the Rolleston Committee heralded the beginning of what is known as the 'British system': the medical profession was given the power and responsibility to define 'addiction' and 'treatment'; the Home Office, however, rather than the Ministry of Health, retained a residual administrative power. In terms of the subtle interrelation between the two models of drug use within the deterrence perspective (medical and moral-legal), Virginia Berridge makes the following revealing observations of the situation after 1926. Having noted that the 'moderate stable addict' was largely a 'casualty' of the disease theory generally, and emphasizing again its hybrid quality, she writes:

> The Rolleston Report did not simply mark a victory for the 'medical model' of addiction *per se*. . . . A distinctive medical ideology of addiction operated through and with government policy towards narcotics. . . . The moral emphasis of the disease theory was carried over into the new era of addiction as a social problem, addiction as social policy. Doctors henceforth were in partnership with the state.[51]

15

In practical terms, initially at least, the 'British system' of medical self-regulation seemed to work well. This was due, however, to the absence of endemic drug use rather than any attribute of the 'system'. 'Drug use did not become a major problem in Britain until the late 1950s and then . . . the British "system" began to break down'.[52] It was a relatively mild increase in the recreational use of drugs in the 1950s, including a noticeable increased use among the 'indigenous population',[53] that precipitated the convening in 1958 of the Ministry of Health Interdepartmental Committee on Drug Addiction to undertake a policy review. Also named after its chairman, this was the first 'Brain Committee'. Its 1961 report affirmed the view of the Rolleston Committee that addiction was basically a medical matter: it should be regarded 'as an expression of mental disorder rather than a form of criminal behaviour'.[54] It also noted that the incidence of addiction remained small, with two predominant classes of addicts: members of the medical and pharmaceutical professions and 'therapeutic addicts'. The Brain Committee concluded that there should be no major departure from the recommendations of the Rolleston Committee.

As elsewhere, however, drug-use patterns changed dramatically during the 1960s. Cannabis, amphetamine, and LSD became increasingly popular, and addiction to heroin also increased.[55] Media attention and legislative concern led to a reconvening of the Brain Committee. Although the committee's second report in 1965 again affirmed the medical nature of the matter – 'the addict should be regarded as a sick person, he should be treated as such and not as a criminal, provided he does not resort to criminal acts'[56] – drug policy was no longer explicitly seen *solely* in terms of treatment of individual addicts.[57] The 1965 report reformulated the medical model to emphasize control as well as individual treatment: addiction was also a 'socially infectious condition'.[58] Thus, the 'partnership' between the medical profession and the state which Berridge had regarded as implicit after 1926 was made plain at this stage. Noting the increased use of various drugs and the increase in heroin addiction, and given that there was a negligible traffic in illicit heroin (and little prescription forgery), it was obvious that the major source of supply for the increased heroin use was a small minority of doctors who had prescribed excessively for addicts.[59] Recognizing that a complete ban on heroin would have opened up the possibility of an extensive black market trade, the prescribing of heroin and cocaine to addicts was taken out of the hands of general medical practitioners and made the task of specialist hospital doctors; general practitioners were allowed to continue to prescribe these drugs to 'ordinary patients' only.[60] This new 'clinic system', which also incorporated a system of compulsory notification of addicts, began in April 1968.

The revision of British drug policy after the second Brain Report did not incorporate all drugs: 'the focus was on narcotics and the multiple drug use of many people largely went unremarked. . . . The consequence of this narrowly focused approach was to leave responses to the use of other drugs either to the discretion of individual doctors or to legal sanctions.'[61] Although harm reduction at the level of local services remains a vital aspect of drug policy in Britain, this 'narrowly-focused approach' left the way open, at the level of political policy, for the gradual escalation of a war on drugs in the American style. Referring to the abject failure of the moral-legal model to significantly reduce the high levels of illicit drug use in the United States, David Downes remarks of this process that '. . . the trajectory of narcotics control in Britain is converging rapidly with that of the United States. The least successful model of narcotics control is proving the most influential.'[62]

When illicit drug use first came to the attention of the Irish authorities in the mid-1960s with the emergence of sporadic instances of amphetamine, cannabis, and LSD use,[63] it led, in 1968, to the establishment of a special Drug Squad in the Garda Síochána. A Working Party on Drug Abuse was established under the Department of Health in the same year. The Working Party reported in 1971[64] and the Misuse of Drugs Act 1977 was the legislative result. This legislation creates the category of 'controlled drugs' – any substance, product or preparation that is specified in the Schedule to the Act (which may be ministerially altered).[65] Possession of controlled drugs, except under limited circumstances (e.g. in the case of a medical practitioner or pharmacist), is an offence.[66] It is provided that the Minister for Health, for the purpose of preventing the misuse of controlled drugs, may make regulations regarding the manufacture, production, preparation, importation, exportation, supply, offering to supply, distribution, or transportation of controlled drugs, and also concerning the prescription of controlled drugs.[67] Special procedures to prevent irresponsible prescribing are set out in detail.[68] A system of scaled offences was introduced, with cannabis offences relating to personal use subjected to lighter penalties.[69] It was also provided that, in most cases, courts should place convicted prisoners on remand while a medical report was prepared; in certain cases, the court was to arrange for the medical treatment and care of such persons.[70]

However, as has been noted by Shane Butler (in a comprehensive review of Irish drug policy from which the following discussion benefits greatly), the 1971 report lacks any analysis of exactly what is meant by 'drug abuse', it is assumed that it is a self-evident social problem.[71] It is also assumed that supply-reduction and abstinence are the only policy options. Butler notes of this period that, within the Department of Health, responsibility for drug problems was assigned to the Food and Drugs Section (now renamed the Community Health Division) rather than to the Mental Health Section: 'the effect of this, consciously or otherwise, was to ensure an emphasis on drug control systems rather than care systems'.[72] While advocating that drug education should develop as an integral part of the school curriculum, being taught by teachers in the context of religious education, health education or civics, 'the working party did not apply similar "normalisation" principles to its recommendations on treatment services for drug users and drug addicts'.[73] Instead, it advocated that treatment and rehabilitation should be specialized rather than delivered as part of primary care services or within the newly developing community mental health services.

The initial 'drugs crisis' subsided by the late 1970s and data (from the National Drug Advisory and Treatment Centre at Jervis Street in Dublin and Garda crime statistics) indicated that the 'drug problem' was confined to the use of cannabis and LSD. The 'opiate epidemic' which developed in Dublin between 1980 and 1984, however, transformed this situation. The intravenous use of heroin increased dramatically, and petty theft to support expensive drug habits as well as organized commercial drug dealing became common.[74] The Jervis Street Centre treated 55 heroin users in 1979, in 1980 this rose to 213, and in 1981 to 417.[75] In April 1983, a Special Governmental Task Force on Drug Abuse in the Department of Health was established.

Although the Task Force report was not published, it was later leaked. It contained a section devoted to 'Community and Youth Development'; this was 'the clearest and most explicit acknowledgement ever made by Irish policy makers that drug problems in Dublin were largely explicable in terms of the poverty and powerlessness of a small number of working-class neighbourhoods'.[76] On this basis, it suggested the identification of 'Community Priority Areas' which would receive extra resources and services coordinated by a 'Youth and Community Development Forum'. As Butler notes, however, the Department of Health press release on the report completely ignored these aspects:

> It cannot, however, be too strongly stressed that in this
> area, above all others, it is the individual decision which
> counts most. The decision not to experiment with hard
> drugs is one which any individual can make before he
> becomes hooked.[77]

The actual result of the work of this group was the Misuse of Drugs Act 1984. This legislation reflected the definitive adoption, at the political level, of the 'moral-legal' view of drug use: higher fines and harsher sentences for drug offences were introduced,[78] and the mandatory requirement in the 1977 legislation that the court remand certain convicted prisoners while awaiting a medical report was replaced by an optional arrangement, depending on whether the court considered it appropriate or not.[79]

As regards treatment services, there followed a period of confusion and conflict between the statutory bodies – the Eastern Health Board, the Jervis Street Centre, and the Health Education Bureau – and local community groups. Butler describes how the community groups were demanding money that was 'not there' and also points out that

> philosophically they posed a threat to the *status quo* through their insistence that drug users should be seen, understood and helped in the context of their families and neighbourhoods, rather than seen as having a clinical condition which warranted treatment at a centralised facility at a considerable remove from their usual environment.[80]

At the state level, on the other hand,

> It would not be accurate to say that [the] 'harm-reduction' perspective was rejected by Irish policy makers; rather would it be more accurate to say that there is no evidence that it was ever discussed at any level, that policy makers may have been largely unaware of it, and that American ideas of the need for an all-out 'War on Drugs' were taken as self-evidently right and sufficient.[81]

The Task Force had recommended that a new National Coordinating Committee on Drug Abuse be established and this was done in early 1985. At the services level, some harm-reduction approaches had been developed in Ireland, as elsewhere, largely due to the acknowledgement that intravenous drug users were in a 'high-risk' category in terms of contracting the AIDS virus. Methadone maintenance and needle-exchange schemes, as well as 'Outreach' programmes, were all developed during this period, representing the end of complete abstinence goals (where these existed). The 1991 *Government Strategy* appears to endorse these practical movements in the direction of harm reduction. It recommends a wider role for general practitioners and the establishment of 'community drug teams'.[82] At the political level, however, the general policy emphasis and the force of the criminal law remain focused on the supply-reduction, demand-reduction, and 'international co-operation' measures which were referred to in the introductory section of this paper. As Butler remarks, the *Government Strategy* is far from a radical departure. He describes it as being 'in its overall tone, an administrator's report rather than a policy maker's report' and as closing debate rather than opening it up.[83] His conclusion is equally clear: 'The consensus which has been a feature of Irish drug policy making has been superficial . . . it has been achieved and maintained by ignoring many real policy dilemmas, and . . . such consensus-seeking may in the long run be of less societal value than an open acknowledgement of institutional conflict and cultural ambivalence'.[84]

Subsequent legislative measures have been oriented solely towards supply reduction. The Criminal Justice Act 1994 makes provision for the recovery of the proceeds of drug trafficking and other offences: money laundering, the means by which criminal proceeds are processed through the financial system and converted into legitimate assets, was made an offence carrying severe penalties. The Criminal Justice (Drug Trafficking) Act 1996 introduces seven-day detention for suspected drug traffickers. Four further pieces of legislation designed to combat the drug-crime nexus were intro-duced in July 1996.[85] This occurred in the wake of the murder of investigative journalist, Veronica Guerin, allegedly by criminals involved in drug trafficking. The public outcry that followed Guerin's murder and the subsequent knee-jerk political response avoided any analysis of the broader issues involved. Crime reduc-tion, rather than harm reduction, became firmly established as state policy towards the perennial human activity of drug-taking.

3. DRUG, SET AND SETTING

This chapter examines an underlying assumption of the deterrence perspective on drug policy: that certain drugs are definitively dangerous and dependence producing or addictive. The main objec-tive is to expose the flaws in the 'medical' model of drug use as a basis for drug policy. The basic point is as follows: all drugs are *relatively* safe and that to describe them as intrinsically dependence producing or addictive is misleading. Although this claim may be counterintuitive, it is by no means novel. It is, in fact, the conclusion of most writers on the subject. Drugs – which are, after all, inert substances – only have the *potential* to be dangerous. This distinction is of the utmost importance. As one writer, for example, remarks of heroin, cocaine, marijuana, and LSD: 'If used responsibly, with due precautions, no harm will come. In contrast, a careless or reckless user may meet disaster.'[86]

The key work underlying this understanding of the use of drugs in the non-medical context is Norman Zinberg's *Drug, Set, and Setting: The Basis for Controlled Intoxicant Use*, published in 1984.[87] This book (and, indeed, all of Zinberg's work) is notable both for the extensiveness of his research and the responsible approach that he adopts in this complex area. Zinberg's central idea – developed after careful interviews with users of marijuana, heroin and LSD – is that 'in order to understand what impels someone to use an illicit drug and how that drug affects the user, three determinants must be considered: drug (the pharmacologic action of the substance itself), set (the attitude of the person at the time of use, including his personality structure), and setting (the influence of the physical and social setting within which the use occurs)'.[88] The effect of any drug, in other words, is not a constant; instead, it is a variable within certain limits, depending on the interrelationship between the personality of the drug taker, the context or environment in which the drug is consumed, and the drug itself. As Zinberg writes:

> The relationships among personality (set), social structure (setting), and drug initially seem obvious. Everyone knows that psychic states vary greatly, that the environment affects them, and that drugs may make a tremendous impact on them. But these relationships, though easy to grasp in theory, are surprisingly difficult to accept as specific conditions. Thus we wrongly assume that the effect of a drug is constant . . .[89]

This is not to suggest that drug effects should not be considered at all in the discussion about drugs, or, for example, that stimulants like cocaine or amphetamine are as likely to leave the user in a lethargic state as an activated one. It is rather to emphasize that any assertion of a *precise* and *regular* relationship between chemical substances and particular human behaviour or reactions is misleading. In this connection, Zinberg gives the example of alcohol: 'From the standpoint of pharmacology, alcohol suppresses the action of certain inhibitors in the brain and can have no result inconsistent with this action. Yet the range of actual effects in terms of both behavioral change and psychic state is extremely wide.'[90]

Zinberg's general analysis pays particular attention to drug 'setting', the determinant in drug use that had previously received the least recognition. He argues that it is the social setting, through the development of social controls, that determines the nature and extent of drug use. 'The use of any drug involves both values and rules of conduct [social sanctions] and patterns of behavior [social rituals]; these two together are known as informal social controls.'[91] Social sanctions 'define whether and how a particular drug should be used', and social rituals are 'the stylized, prescribed behavior patterns surrounding the use of a drug'.[92]

Zinberg's main policy recommendation is that every possible effort – legally, medically, and socially – should be made to distinguish between 'the two basic types of psychoactive drug consumption: that which is experimental, recreational and circumstantial, and therefore has minimal social costs ['drug use']; and that which is dysfunctional, intensified and compulsive, and therefore has high social costs ['drug misuse' or 'drug abuse']'.[93] Zinberg argues that greater attention should be paid by policy makers to the conditions of use rather than to the prevention of use. This suggestion is the essence of harm-reduction strategies; it does not mean that the goal of prevention should be abandoned entirely, but that 'emphasis should be shifted away from the prevention of all use to the prevention of dysfunctional use'.[94]

There can be no doubt as to the validity of Zinberg's distinction. Drug use – whether of heroin, cocaine, marijuana, or any other drug – can be innocuous. As David Richards has commented:

> Humans use drugs for diverse purposes – for thera-
> peutic care and cure, for relief of pain or anxiety, for
> stimulation or depression of moods, for exploration of
> imaginative experience (for creative, aesthetic, religious,
> therapeutic, or other reasons), for recreative pleasure,
> and the like. Humans consciously choose among these

purposes depending on the context and their individual aims. . . . For many, such drug use does not constitute fear-ridden anarchy, but promotes the rational self-control of those ingredients fundamental to the design of a fulfilled life.[95]

Indicating still other types of use, Jara Krivanek has stated that 'One can use drugs to assert one's autonomy or masculinity, claim adult status, express conviviality, identify with a group, manifest group solidarity and engage in a host of other actions that human beings generally regard as important and personally satisfying.'[96] The deterrence perspective on drug policy, however, does not in practice countenance the use–misuse distinction. The 1991 *Government Strategy*, for example, is based solely on a definition of 'drug misuse': 'the taking of a legal and/or illegal drug or drugs (excluding alcohol and tobacco) which harm the physical, mental or social well-being of the individual, the group or society'.[97] The legal arrangements supported by the 1991 report, in turn, are based on a presumption of this misuse. The result is *overcriminalization*: the use of prohibited drugs, in cases where no 'harm' results, continues to be criminalized by virtue of the fact that the mere sale or possession of these drugs constitute offences. Central to the medico-moral views on drug use which underlie this criminalization is the classic image of dysfunctional drug use: drug addiction.

'Addiction' originally referred to a process of Roman Law whereby a thing or a person was formally made over to another person in order to discharge a debt.[98] When Benjamin Rush chose to use the term in his 1785 formulation of 'alcohol addiction' as a 'disease of the will', the ground was laid for the 'addictive' quality of certain substances to become the basis for the medical model of drug use that developed during the nineteenth century. Assuming some degree of predisposition, gradual or abrupt loss of control over use and progression, the disease theory of addiction remains, particularly with regard to treatment, highly influential. The theory, however, is coming under increasing challenge. Apart from the fact that medicine itself is 'confused about diseases',[99] there is, in the present context, no consensus as to what 'drug addiction' exactly involves or as to how it should be 'treated'; it is 'a complex phenomenon which has generated a good deal of heat and invited much speculation, but which continues to defy understanding and analysis as fast as it grows'.[100] Indeed, the expression 'drug addiction' itself has been rejected as unsuitable by the Expert Committee on Addiction-producing Drugs of the World Health Organisation (WHO). This body made its first formal attempt to define addiction in 1952; it clarified this in 1958 by distinguishing between 'addiction' and 'habit', but both terms were finally abandoned in favour of 'drug dependence' in 1964. The more recent 1981 WHO definition of 'drug dependence' is worth quoting at length, precisely to highlight the ambiguity admitted even at that level:

> Drug dependence is a syndrome manifested by a behavioral pattern in which the use of a given psychoactive drug, or class of drugs, is given a much higher priority than other behaviors that once had a higher value. . . . The dependence syndrome is not absolute, but it is a quantitive phenomenon that exists in different degrees . . . no sharp cut-off point can be identified for distinguishing drug dependence from non-dependent but recurrent drug use. At the extreme, the dependence syndrome is associated with 'compulsive drug-using behavior'. Dependence on drugs is not always a major disability. The drug can cause little tissue damage, little impairment of function, and be relatively inexpensive. . . . Not every individual who experiences impairment or disability relating to drug consumption is suffering from drug dependence.[101]

This definition, while it gives some sense as to the nature of addiction, remains limited. As Krivanek notes, 'drug dependence' will take some time to catch on as a replacement expression.[102] The equivocal aspects of the 'syndrome' are apparent in that drug use and drug dependence are not readily distinguishable and the element of progression is left open to question. This general lack of certainty regarding the phenomenon is further disclosed in that the implications for treatment are unclear from this definition.

Specifically undermining the medical model is the research that revealed how several American soldiers, while serving in Vietnam, had become addicted to heroin, a substance that was relatively cheap and easily available in south-east Asia.[103] The vast majority of these soldiers managed to adjust easily to a non-drug lifestyle on their return to the United States.[104] Krivanek also refers to the general evidence 'that some former addicts return to regular but controlled and non-addictive use'.[105] These problems with the 'medical' approach are made forcefully by Stanton Peele:

> A crucial element in the disease myth of addiction, one used to justify expensive, long-term – and increasingly coercive and involuntary – treatment is the progressive and irreversible nature of addiction. . . . All data dispute this. Epidemiological research finds that people typically outgrow drinking problems. . . . The data on drug abuse are identical. . . .[106]

Applying the three determinants of 'drug', 'set' and 'setting' to the longer term, it is clear that the habit-forming potential of a drug, as well as the effect, is variable. The drugs 'supply an element of leisure, comfort, relief, satisfaction or confidence, but the driving force towards dependence lies in the psyche of the user'.[107] Addiction, therefore, 'is not a property of drugs at all. . . . Addiction is a property of the user'.[108] The user, in turn, must be viewed in the context of his or her social environment. There should be no question of the 'drug' determinant being accorded a priority it does not deserve; drugs 'merely have particular effects, and even these may vary considerably from one person to another. The use of [labels such as 'good' and 'bad'] requires not so much a knowledge of the drugs' actions but the adoption of a particular set of values'.[109] Drugs, in short, are an 'invalid variable' in addiction:

> A person's needs, not the drugs, determine the possi-
> bility and power of addiction. The more needs a drug
> meets, the stronger the addiction. Those needs, not the
> drugs, must be addressed in order to reduce the amount
> of drug use and addiction.[110]

The major failing of the medical model is its orientation away from the 'needs' of individuals and the role that these play in substance use and misuse. By looking to individual needs and the social and psychological circumstances in which they occur, it becomes apparent that the most appropriate way to approach various forms of dependence is to see them essentially as *learned behaviours* rather than as 'conditions' of any kind. There is no doubt as to the existence of forms of drug dependence: addiction is simply better understood as a product of social learning – a function of 'set' and 'setting' – rather than as a 'disease'.

Social-learning theory, by recognizing various levels of learning, provides a language in which problem drug behaviour can be properly understood. The example of problematic alcohol use is helpful here. Traditionally, as illustrated by the preceding chapter, it has been thought that there is 'certainly a disease called alcoholism, characterised by a person's inability to control intake . . . [it] involves physical and psychological dependence'.[111] As R.E. Kendell, however, in an important challenge to the disease theory of alcoholism based on aspects of the above discussion, noted: 'most of the assumptions of the "disease model" are unjustified and act as a barrier to a more intelligent and effective approach to the problem'.[112] Social-learning theory is the basis for the psychosocial paradigm of 'problem drinking', a paradigm that has effectively superseded 'alcoholism'.[113] This is a learned behavioural disorder which has been defined as 'the repetitive use of beverage alcohol causing physical, psychological or social harm to the drinker or to others'.[114] According to Nick Heather and Ian Robertson, the learning of 'problem drinking' can take place at the following levels: classical conditioning; instrumental learning; modelling; self-management/self-regulation; and higher cognitive processes.[115]

Despite the fact that Irish people consume less alcohol than the European average and spend no more on alcohol than people in most other countries, there is clearly a national image of heavy drinking. It has been argued that the profound ambivalence of Irish people to alcohol – as revealed by the patterns and visibility of Irish alcohol consumption – results in the great prevalence of alcohol problems in Ireland.[116] This ambivalence and resultant behaviour are not primarily medical questions; on the contrary, the ambivalence contributes, at different 'levels' and varying from individual to individual, to social learning. There are obviously many other contributory factors: John Waters has offered a view of problem drinking in Ireland, for example, that might be termed 'psychocultural':

> If there were psychiatrists' couches for peoples and societies Ireland would long since have been diagnosed as an alcoholic nation. We like to fool ourselves by thinking of drink as a social lubricant, but its main function in Ireland is as an analgesic. . . . We use it to enter the joyous, creative and resourceful aspects of our personality, to escape the self-loathing which results from centuries of abuse.[117]

Waters goes on to argue convincingly, in the context of a discussion on the popularity of Ecstasy among Irish young people and the resistance to strict drink-driving laws in Ireland, that to treat the former drug as a 'scourge' and alcohol – 'a more consistently lethal one – as a harmless social lubricant is an act of criminal hypocrisy and denial'.[118] Ecstasy can also be lethal, of course; the question, however, is whether this potential property, which legal drugs also possess, is enough to merit its demonization. In a recent Irish medical journal article on Ecstasy, a group of psychiatrists noted that 'it is often forgotten that drug misuse in adolescence can be secondary to emotional disturbance' and that emotional disturbance can be seen as a 'possible aetiological factor' in cases of drug misuse.[119] In non-medical language: such 'emotional disturbance' is another factor in social learning. In reality, the focus on the drug as a 'scourge' often serves as a convenient means of avoiding other, less comfortable, questions.

Both the psychosocial and sociocultural models of drug use incorporate aspects of social-learning theory. As regards learning processes in *non-problematic drug use*, Norman Zinberg's ideas of social sanctions and social rituals are usually given importance. Zinberg describes these learned controls as including: definitions of moderate use; condemnation of compulsive use; identification of potentially untoward drug effects; and the precautions to be taken before and during use.[120] In a more recent paper, Zinberg made the following explicit reference to the legalization debate:

> The development of social sanctions and rituals prob-
> ably occurs more slowly in the secretive world of illicit
> drug use than with the use of a licit drug like alcohol.
> The furtiveness, the suspicion, the fears of legal reprisal,
> as well as the myths and misconceptions that surround
> illicit drug use, all make the exchange of information
> [i.e. learning] that leads to the development of social
> sanctions and controls more difficult.[121]

In other words, the use of drugs is *more likely* to become misuse under the circumstances created by a war on drugs.

As regards learning processes in *problematic drug behaviour*, the focus is on misadaptation to society. The precise reasons why, and the means by which, destructive drug behaviour is 'learned' are multifarious. I have already referred to ambivalence towards alcohol, Waters' 'psychoculturalism', and emotional disturbance. Research also shows a correlation between substance misuse and a history of sexual or physical abuse.[122] Further, and perhaps most significantly, economic factors (and their social consequences) are repeatedly shown to play a very significant and direct role in the learning of some individuals. Where there exists disadvantage in these terms, substance dependence can more easily become meaningful and, in due course, learned. In this view, families living in socially dis-advantaged conditions are sometimes described as 'necessarily [instilling] in their children things like weak ego functioning, defective superego, inadequate masculine identification, lack of appropriate aspirations and a failure to set long-range goals, as well as a distrust of traditional social institutions'.[123] Drug use, therefore, 'is seen as part of a pattern of substitute gratification'.[124] In 1994, for example, 'the most probable profile' of the problem drug user who came to a treatment centre in the Greater Dublin area was that of 'a young, poorly educated, unemployed male, living in a deprived area and misusing heroin'.[125] As has been remarked in the Irish context generally: 'Even if we make due allowance for the fact that the addictive nature of the drugs may to some extent create the demand, what we are dealing with is social situations that generate the need for the kinds of escapism that drugs offer.'[126]

When drug problems are perceived in this sense of 'learned behaviour', it is clear that the criminal prohibition of drugs, in the limited way that it deters or prevents drug use, merely acts as a diversion for problematic behaviour. One group of writers makes this point in the following way: 'making [drugs] inaccessible may only result in an increase in other health-damaging behaviours which serve the same function [as the drug-taking]. It is possible that these behaviours could be more harmful and less easy to monitor or control'.[127]

The question remains as to the appropriate responses to these behaviours. Different views exist in the normalization perspective: whereas the psychosocial model of drug use tends to view addiction as 'a pattern of maladaptive, learned habits that are modifiable by cognitive and behavioral techniques',[128] in the sociocultural model the learned habits are modifiable by interventions at the broader, environmental level. In the authentic version of the psychosocial model, treatment of the individual drug user – avoiding the medico-moral ideologies of the deterrence perspective – is seen as the primary means of intervention.[129] In the sociocultural model, which is the model that I am favouring as the appropriate guide for political-legal policy, 'attention must be focused on the state and social structures which play a part in the individual's adaptation to society' and interventions aimed at modifying destructive drug behaviours 'are required to penetrate culture and the psychology of the individual'.[130] These themes will now be taken up in a discussion of the moral dimensions of the war on drugs.

4. DRUGS, MORALITY AND THE CRIMINAL SANCTION

This chapter relates particularly to the moral-legal model of drug use, the cornerstone of the war on drugs. From the analytical and expositional point of view, it is at this stage that the complexity of drug policy becomes most apparent. Although the moral-legal and medical models have been historically entwined, some of the issues raised by them are markedly distinct. It is therefore necessary to make some preliminary observations before indicating precisely how this chapter builds on the foundations laid down in chapter 3.

There are many facets to the relationship between drugs, drug policy and morality. One distinction which is often made in this regard is between, on the one hand, the 'moral' aspects of the issue and, on the other hand, the 'technical' or 'practical' points of view.[131] This dichotomy, however, is far from straightforward. Morality is a reference to feelings which people have about right and wrong, or good and bad. At the general level, when any social policy is examined, the examination is a moral one. That is to say, there is a broad, or 'social', moral issue at stake. As Morris Ginsberg has remarked, in a statement which applies to policy as much as to law: 'The ultimate justification of law is that it serves moral ends. . . . I know of no attempt to free law from morals which does not in the long run, consciously or unconsciously, reintroduce ethical principles.'[132] This issue of 'social morality' is present in drug policy (and law) as much as it exists in very different policy questions such as abortion, taxation rates, or social welfare.[133] The broad moral question of this pamphlet can be phrased as follows: 'Is current drug policy – as manifested in the legal prohibition of certain drugs – right or wrong?' I am arguing that it is wrong. I regard prohibition as ineffectual, irresponsible, and illegitimate: it is ineffectual because it is falling far short of its objectives; it is irresponsible because it is contributing, directly and indirectly, to the creation of greater social problems than those which it is directed against; and it is illegitimate because it employs incarceration and other criminal sanctions in an improper and excessive manner.

It is impossible, in turn, to conceive of any of these three specific claims in terms that are either purely 'technical' or purely 'moral'. They are all value-laden claims in that they incorporate *standards* (of effectiveness, responsibility and legitimacy of state action). They also include technical elements, notably the extent of 'social dam-age' and the degree of 'harm', both actual and potential, that drugs (or prohibition) cause. Clearly, there is enormous difficulty here in relation to quantification: 'All statistics are imperfect, but those related to drug use are egregiously bad.'[134] The extent of illicit drug consumption, whether it be use or misuse, can only be estimated crudely; in addition, any 'harm' is often of a purely interpersonal kind. Also, 'measurement' will invariably involve moral judgement as to the force, in terms of the broader argument, to be given to various harms.

The moral and practical aspects of this issue cannot, therefore, be easily disentangled. For the purposes of convenience, however, some distinctions must be made. Accordingly, I will reserve my argument that current drug policy is ineffectual and irresponsible until the next chapter. Both of these matters lend themselves to a more empirical approach than the question that will be addressed in this chapter: the legitimacy of state action concerning drugs. The argument presented in chapter 3 was that drug use and problematic drug use should be perceived in behavioural terms, as functions of psychological and social factors, rather than in medical terms. It is my contention that the legitimacy of current drug policy is under-mined when these psychological and social factors relating to drug use, as well as certain other social and cultural processes, are explored and placed in context. First, however, it is necessary to refer to (and dispense with) a more traditional method of ascer-taining the legitimacy or otherwise of criminal legislation.

The legitimate scope of the criminal law is an extremely contentious jurisprudential issue. John Stuart Mill's 'harm principle' is often invoked in the context of various voluntary acts and con-ducts that have been decriminalized in several jurisdictions, such as abortion, homosexual behaviour, and euthanasia.[135] This principle — that the only purpose for which power can be rightfully exercised over any member of a community against his or her will is to prevent harm to others – is also of relevance to the drug prohibition debate. Since drug use is conduct that does not *directly* harm others, there is the view that such conduct should be protected by Mill's libertarian principle. The opposing view to that of Mill is characterized as a Platonic 'philosopher-king perspective'.[136] James Fitzjames Stephen, Mill's leading nineteenth-century opponent, noted an 'enormous mass of bad and indifferent people' in the world, and considered it the duty of the state to actively promote, and indeed enforce, a particular conception of 'the good'.[137] The 'philosopher-king perspective' corresponds to the moral-legal model of drug use – the view which condemns all illicit drug use as wrong. In terms of developments in the criminal law generally, it should be noted that moral ideology of this kind is losing ground. The leading English textbook on criminal law, for example, states that there are two characteristics that were traditionally found in acts which are crimes: 'a public wrong' (acts which have a particularly harmful effect on the public and do more than interfere with merely private rights) and 'a moral wrong'.[138] In relation to the latter, the authors note that 'now many acts are prohibited on the grounds of social expediency and not because of their immoral nature' and that 'the test of immorality is not a very helpful one. . . . The enforcement of morality . . . by the criminal law is losing ground.'[139]

In the present context, the essential point is that the discourse initiated by Mill and Stephen lacks specificity. Neither theoretical perspective can be conclusive:

> Whether the imponderable element is the responsi-
> bility of the government for character formation or the
> freedom of adults to choose their own habits and seek
> their own destiny, the admixture of these elements with
> others that are at least in principle measurable renders
> the claims of both parties logically unassailable.[140]

At a superficial level, we can interpret Mill's 'harm principle' to include 'victimless' conduct; that interpretation, however, in terms of a practical application, merely begs further questions. The consumption of a drug is a personal act with immediate consequences only for the consumer, yet there is at least the potential for external effects which can include harm to others of various kinds. As William Binchy has remarked of this perennial conundrum, 'Human beings cannot function outside society: the social dimension is as inevitable a characteristic of individual human experience as is the most private and intimate of our thoughts and activities.'[141] The essential question, in terms of each specific policy debate, is the interpretation to be given to this notion of 'social dimension'. In the present context, this question brings us back to the issue of the factors underlying the different forms of drug use. To put this another way: how does the broad social context of drug use impact on the question of the legitimacy of the criminal prohibition of drugs? If we live in a society that not only witnesses but also *cultivates* drug use and misuse, is it acceptable for the state to criminalize drug-related behaviour and activity?

In my view, the fundamental difficulty with the moral argument that drug use is wrong is that it perceives that use (or misuse) as existing in a social vacuum, with effects moving outward from it, rather than seeing it as a phenomenon in symbiosis with the wider culture. In other words, just as with the medical model, there is no serious attempt to comprehend or assess the manifest *need* for drugs throughout society. The remainder of this chapter will make such an attempt. Reference will first be made to socioeconomic considerations. These, however, form only a part of the picture: there are obviously other, more general, processes at play in the drug dynamic – a 'dynamic' that incorporates high levels of consumption and criminalization that I consider to be unjustified. I will frame my discussion of these other factors in the light of the non-applicability of traditional left–right political ideologies to the full scope of the drugs debate.

Traditional political ideology is not, of course, completely irrelevant. I have already indicated that much of the need for drugs must be perceived in terms of social and economic deprivation: as the official evidence that was referred to in the last chapter makes clear, drug problems are directly related to present economic structures of power and exploitation. These structures are no less a part of the moral framework within which drug use must be seen than the effects of the drugs themselves. The tendency to ignore the roles of these factors is by no means a new development: Gerry Johnstone, for example, in his study of the relation between medical and moral concerns in the nineteenth-century Inebriety Movement, notes that medical discourses individualized the problem of deviance

> not by reducing it to biological defect but by insisting
> that it was ultimately caused by personal immorality.
> Ergo, behaviour that was often an inevitable consequence
> of living in appalling social conditions was portrayed, in
> medical discourse, as a consequence of the individual's
> lack of discipline.[142]

At the same time, however, there is greater political and moral complexity involved in the drugs issue than the fundamental social policy contradiction that present patterns of economic distribution will lead inevitably to destructive behaviours like drug misuse and, indeed, to prohibition-related criminal activity. Although, in the case of certain drugs, there are identifiable patterns of use and misuse, the fact remains that illicit and licit drugs, including pharmaceutical drugs, are misused by members of all classes or 'groups'. Thus, while treated opiate misuse is largely confined to poorer and educationally disadvantaged groups, there is little evidence, for example, that the use or misuse of cannabis and Ecstasy is similarly concentrated in any particular section of the community. In addition, instances of cocaine misuse have traditionally been more confined to the wealthier groups in society. As Neil Boyd and John Lowman have remarked, 'given the occurrence of drug use at all levels of society, it will take much more than poverty to explain the phenomenon of drug use and shape policies designed to deal with abuse'.[143]

The other contributory factors to learning drug-dependent behaviour that were mentioned in the last chapter – including emotional disturbance, and sexual or physical abuse – are present in all sections of the community. In a moment, I will argue that there are other *social and cultural processes* that are related closely to patterns of drug use and learned drug dependence. These processes, which are general and in no sense group-specific, are also a part of the broad moral framework within which drug use must be understood.

Before discussing these processes, and indeed, by way of introducing them, it is important to recognize that the many different types of drugs and drug users mean that easy categorization of the issues involved, in terms of traditional left–right politics, is impossible. The values assumed by the deterrence model are certainly conservative: that the present social and economic organization of Western society is preferable to any possible or likely alternatives and that difficulties in the functioning of that organization are aberrational (and thus susceptible to an abstract 'exclusion') rather than endemic (and thus necessarily 'integrated'). Nonetheless, despite the fact that 'drugs' clearly do not constitute an autonomous 'social problem' that can somehow be resolved by *specific* drug-policy measures, there has been no concerted opposition to the dominant war on drugs ideology from the political left. The reasons underlying this conservative consensus include (in addition to the complicating multiplicity of social groups involved), the highly effective demonization of illicit drugs and the traditional centrality of (unaltered) consciousness to socialist politics.

It is illuminating, in the light of these considerations, to place the drugs issue in the broad context of the contemporary 'post-socialist' political landscape. This landscape includes the demands for 'recognition of difference' on the part of national, ethnic, 'race', gender, and sexual groups, and the demands for socioeconomic redistribution which they have in many senses supplanted as the key platforms for social struggle. Many of the collectivities which are active in this 'post-socialist' sense have been described as 'bivalent': they are 'differentiated as collectivities by virtue of *both* the political-economic structure *and* the cultural-valuational structure of society . . . [and therefore] implicated simultaneously in both the politics of redistribution and the politics of recognition'.[144] Although there is an absence of any recognized collectivity in relation to drug use, this bivalency is nonetheless present at one level. Those citizens who are criminalized due to drug prohibition (a criminalization that I consider to be unjust) are also implicated in these two different forms of politics: some by virtue of the socioeconomic conditions underlying their use, others because of their 'different' decision to use drugs, and others still by some combination of these.

The observations of Nancy Fraser with regard to the different means of attempting to remedy injustices, whether motivated by 'redistribution' or 'recognition', are particularly relevant. Fraser suggests that there are two distinct types of remedies.[145] 'Affirmation remedies' are aimed at correcting inequitable outcomes of social arrangements without disturbing the underlying framework that generates them. In terms of patterns of economic distribution, this implies liberal welfarism; as regards recognition of difference or identity, it involves policies based on mainstream multiculturalism. 'Transformation remedies', on the other hand, are aimed at correcting inequitable outcomes by restructuring the underlying generative framework. The connection between Fraser's analysis and the war on drugs lies in the fact that 'transformation remedies' involve responses to social problems generally that are precisely those implied, in my view, by the 'sociocultural' model of drug use: socialist redistribution, and deconstruction.

I have already made reference to the politics of distribution. That argument cannot be overemphasized: quite simply, present patterns of distribution seriously undermine the moral argument for the prohibition of drugs; socioeconomic restructuring is essential if present drug misuse related to poverty, unemployment and educational disadvantage is to be properly addressed. This is one element of the necessary 'penetration of culture' that was referred to at the close of the last chapter. Deconstruction is the other, very different, element. It provides the framework within which the general *social and cultural processes* that underlie drug use, and undermine the condemnation of that use, can be assessed. Thus, it also acts as a 'remedy' to the failures and injustice of the war on drugs.

The contemporary usage of the term 'deconstruction' refers to the work of the French philosopher, Jacques Derrida. Although originally conceived as a set of philosophical practices regarding the interpretation of texts, deconstructive techniques now play investigative and normative roles in diverse aspects of social theory, including legal and political theory. Derrida himself is now part of the group of 'postmodern writers' who, generally speaking, 'having had enough of signs and texts, . . . are now concentrating on law and legitimation'.[146] In legal and political theory, deconstruction can be understood, again in general terms, as a 'process of exposing or undoing the assumptions implicit in an argument'.[147] In the words of Jack Balkin:

> Legal doctrines both reflect and regulate social life. The choice of protected rights and of enforcement techniques reflect views, whether obvious or obscure, about social relations. Law tells a story about what people are and should be. . . . Too often we forget that our systems of law are based upon metaphor and interpretation; we mistake the dominant or privileged vision of people and society for real 'present' human nature. . . . At that point, the metaphor becomes mistaken for what it

> describes. But latent within the metaphor is a counter-
> vision that can be located and brought to the surface
> through deconstruction. It exists within the privileged
> conception because the latter ultimately depends upon
> it in a relation of *différance*.[148]

A basic deconstructive strategy, therefore, involves the identification of ideological hierarchies, and a reversal of the hierarchy for the purposes of destabilization, insight, and perhaps change. There is nothing inevitable about where deconstruction will lead: 'it offers the possibility (and that is all it is) of decentering conventional wisdom.'[149] Deconstruction does require, however, a questioning stance as opposed to a self-righteous or absolutist position.

As in the case of other social injustice, deconstruction aims to transform the 'underlying cultural–valuational structure' of the war on drugs by changing '*everyone's* sense of belonging, affiliation, and self'.[150] Although it is not possible to categorize neatly the hierarchical oppositions inherent in the war on drugs ideology, various repressed ideas and 'countervisions' are not difficult to identify. As for the visions of the law: late capitalist consumerism, the individualistic ethos of the enterprise culture, the glorification of certain types of pleasure and success – all of these facets of contemporary existence are implicated in a thorough analysis of the so-called drug 'menace'. Deconstruction, in essence, counters the certitude and 'necessity' of current drug ideology; it demands, in my view, acknowledgement that drug behaviour, particularly when much of it is innocuous, should not be made the object of the criminal sanction. Deconstruction will not 'solve' any 'drug problem'; its insights, however, will pave the way for an improvment on the present fiasco.

In terms, then, of the central theme of this chapter – the moral condemnation of drug use as the basis for its criminalization – this condemnation takes different forms. Each condemnation reflects drug prohibition by drawing, either implicitly or explicitly, on a set of particular beliefs (an ideology) about morality itself and about illicit drugs. I will attempt to address – and deconstruct – the more significant of these ideologies in the remainder of this chapter.

Many moral objections to drug use reflect a notion developed by Gerald Klerman, the notion of 'pharmacological calvinism';[151] this has been described as 'a general mistrust of drugs used for non-therapeutic purposes and a conviction that if a drug "makes you feel good, it must be morally bad"'.[152] In references to the perceived benefits and pleasures of certain drug use, the objection to 'psycho-tropic hedonism' has been explained as an objection to '. . . the joy of creativity without artistic skill, . . . aesthetic sensibilities without a sense of taste, . . . freedom without responsibility or consequence, . . . self-enchantment without increased complexity, . . . psychotherapy without doubts or anxiety. . .'.[153] Peter Kramer, in his study of the anti-depressant drug, Prozac, notes that the prevailing view as to the nature of pleasure has been that it is a separable result of certain acts.[154] In this view, recreational drug use shortcuts the process: it provides pleasure without the pleasure being 'earned' or 'deserved'. As Kramer writes: 'The concern is that people will pursue pleasure directly . . . rather than achieve pleasure through "distinctly human" intellectual, altruistic, planful efforts for which pleasure is the reward'.[155] Kramer expects Prozac to refocus attention on an alternative theory of pleasure: that it is 'a matter of preference among experiences'.[156] In this view, there is pleasure throughout (and not separable from) certain activities such as reading a book. In response to the idea that the pleasure derived from recreational drugs might apply – through the enhancement or facilitation of other pleasures – to the preference theory, Kramer responds that 'the usual experience-enhancing mood altering drugs, like marijuana or LSD, encourage "self-absorption" and that the experience they enhance is "most often autistic"'.[157] He suggests that Prozac, on the contrary, induces pleasure in part by freeing people –

without inducing distortions of perception – to enjoy activities that are social and productive.

There are some very basic flaws in Kramer's analysis. The pleasurable or other effects of drugs are dependent, as outlined in the preceding chapter, not only on the drug: whether forms of 'self-absorption' or 'autism' are part of the experience of drug use will also depend on 'set' and 'setting'. Thus, for many the experience of Prozac can be very different to the one that he describes, and can even be dangerous. In addition, neither of the two theories of pleasure countenances the variety of ways in which different human beings experience pleasure, and neither looks to the social or personal context in which it is experienced. The limited nature of Kramer's argument is further exposed in another argument – which has its own flaws – against the use of both Ecstasy *and* Prozac. John Drennan writes:

> What makes life fascinating is the struggle to achieve happiness. This can be achieved through work, love, the struggle for friendship or a sense of self worth. Often life can hurt terribly, but it is those experiences that make people special and individual. This is now to be replaced by a pill? Be it Prozac or [Ecstasy], this represents a terrifying vista . . . [Ecstasy] belongs to the sort of amoral society where worth is defined in terms of possessions and cynicism masquerades as critical thought . . .[158]

Again, Drennan totally ignores the relations of production: the notion that unemployment, for example, might strongly incline many people to search for escapist pleasure through drug use is not considered. Moreover, the very cultural processes presently required and created by the capitalist economic order also incline many towards 'escapism'. The consumerist culture, and in particular 'that broad ideological world of modern consumerism' built in part by advertising and its 'images of excitement, achievement, sexuality, youth and pleasure',[159] is based on the creation of a mass non-specifc demand. It is a world 'of plenitude, of gratification without cost, of endless youth'.[160] Drugs are, in these terms, an extremely attractive commodity; in fact, the ideology of waging a 'war' on these commodities in the extremely consumerist environment of late capitalism is, if I might be blunt, laughable. The capitalist market functions to extend consumption and drug use, 'powerfully valued in terms of the hedonism that consumer cultures espouse, is no exception'.[161] John Kaplan has observed that heroin, for example, seems 'almost to have been designed to give trouble to a pluralistic democratic society which lacks massive police resources, maintains a strong tradition of individualism, and values the search for personal pleasure and fulfilment'.[162]

The fact that people can be destructively dependent or 'addicted' to many behaviours and artifacts besides drugs is another issue that is suppressed in the moral perspectives offered by Kramer and Drennan. Other possible 'addictions' include work, power, food, sex, money, television, sport, etc. Indeed, it can be said that capitalism itself cultivates addiction to 'approved' values, such as competition, achievement, and productivity: 'Addiction,' Norman Mailer has written in the context of individuals addicted to money-making processes, 'like faith, is focus from a point of reference.'[163] The deterrence view of drug addiction illustrates, in its narrowly focused vehemence, that our whole attitude toward what might be called 'excessive behaviours' is illogical.[164] *All* addictions can be destructive and damaging.

The rhetoric of the illicit drug 'scourge' must also be placed beside the acquiesence in alcohol and tobacco production and consumption. I have already referred to the phenomenon of 'problem drinking'; the case of the tobacco 'scourge' is no less striking, both in terms of its extensiveness and its geopolitical pattern:

> Tobacco smoking is now generally accepted as the most important cause of premature death, and of much chronic ill-health, in most industrialised countries. In recent years, the habit has been increasing in many developing countries, fostered by ruthless marketing by the multinational tobacco companies.[165]

Another form of moral objection to drugs is represented by the American writer, James Q. Wilson. Drug use, Wilson claims, can 'destroy the user's essential humanity' and 'corrode those natural sentiments of sympathy and duty that constitute our human nature and make possible our social life'.[166] He regards drug dependency as a moral issue and the illegality of certain drugs 'rests in part on their immorality'; legalization would 'undercut', or perhaps 'eliminate altogether', the moral message.[167] Wilson states in another paper:

> The moral reason for attempting to discourage drug use is that the heavy consumption of certain drugs is destructive of human character. These drugs – principally heroin, cocaine, and crack – are, for many people, powerfully reinforcing. The pleasure or oblivion they produce leads many users to devote their lives to seeking pleasure or oblivion and to do so almost regardless of the cost in ordinary human virtues, such as temperance, fidelity, duty, and sympathy.[168]

Wilson is offering arguments against the legalization of drugs that are actually arguments against some possible negative consequences of drug misuse. Any liberalization of the prohibitionist position, in his view, is objected to on grounds of 'drug-dependency' and 'heavy consumption' of specifically mentioned drugs. The most obvious problem with Wilson's statements, in terms of a blanket criminal prohibition, is that the 'heavy consumption' which he describes is merely one form of drug use and is by no means an inevitable consequence of initial use. Again, it is the individual 'set' and the social 'setting' which will dictate whether the initial drug use will lead eventually to the consequences which Wilson treats as consequences of drugs themselves. The drugs mentioned, particularly heroin and cocaine, are not dangerous *per se*. They can be consumed as 'lifestyle choices' without any of the consequences on which Wilson bases his argument. As for the relatively more dangerous crack cocaine, Steven Duke and Albert Gross have argued convincingly that the artificially high costs of cocaine created by prohibition in the United States led to the invention of this more addictive, lower-quality, and less expensive drug, thereby 'democratizing' cocaine.[169] In any system of drug regulation in which harm reduction was the primary goal, consumption of 'crack' could be expected to fall.

Further, Wilson is referring to a type or *style* of 'heavy consumption' found only under a prohibitionist regime, where regular users' lives are necessarily governed by their habit. 'Temperance, fidelity, duty, and sympathy' are under far greater threat when the law of the state criminalizes otherwise voluntary activity. As Ciaran Mc Cullagh has written in the Irish context, to the limited extent that prohibition actually does reduce and 'marginalize' the supply of drugs without reducing demand, these policies have counterproductive effects:

> They increase the price of the remaining drugs thus forcing addicts to make extra income to buy their supply. They can only do this through intensifying their involvement in crime either through increasing their drug-pushing activities or through greater involvement in property crime.[170]

At a deeper level, Wilson's arguments refer to a set of beliefs about the way human nature is constituted. He refers to the destruction, for example, of the user's 'essential humanity'. In the sense that Wilson regards sympathy and duty – aspects of our human nature –

as threatened by drug use, his perspective can be seen as a variation on the themes of temperance and self-control. In Wilson's view of drug use, and indeed in the 'vision' of the law, these are the privileged values; they are privileged over the reality of economic deprivation referred to above, and the other social values that underpin that same deprivation – such as competitiveness and material achievement – are absent from this viewpoint. In the moral condemnation of drug use, the particular conceptions of pleasure and success that are consonant with the enterprise-consumerist culture, and the 'legitimate' means by which they may be achieved – which are often either unavailable or exploitative – are not given a second thought. (For many, of course, participation in the illegal drugs economy is the only feasible entrepreneurial option that presents itself.)

The privileged position of the values of temperance and self-control is also destabilized and threatened by the preference of many for what Stephen Lyng has described as 'experiential anarchy'. Lyng has developed an interesting and relevant perspective on the interaction between the sociological and psychological aspects of 'risk-taking behaviour' generally, including some drug behaviour.[171] His approach seeks to tie together such factors as political economic variables, at one end of the continuum, and individual sensations and feelings, at the other end. Lyng concludes that this behaviour is

> a type of experiential anarchy in which the individual moves beyond the realm of established social patterns to the very fringes of ordered reality. The fact that many people find this type of experience alluring and seek to repeat it as often as possible is an important critical statement on the nature of modern social life.[172]

In relation to drugs, it has also been suggested that many find the very subject of alternative states of consciousness 'menacing in its potential for socially disruptive withdrawal'.[173] Clearly, drug behaviours do have these broad political implications: 'changed states . . . challenge the reigning cultural values. Thus, they may be seen as a threat to the psychological well-being of citizens, particularly to youth but also to the population as a whole, because of our preoccupation with material growth and technological development'.[174]

Drugs do not exist in a social vacuum; they do not constitute an autonomous 'social problem'. They must be viewed in the moral context of social and economic organization generally. The appropriate response to the problems associated with drugs is a multi-sectoral state response, including moves towards socioeconomic redistribution, and also a deconstructive awareness of ambiguity and inherent contradiction in present forms of social organization and social values. As Jara Krivanek has put it, 'If we were really serious about stopping young people from trying drugs, we would have to make some very sweeping changes indeed.'[175] Certainly, under present conditions, the criminal prohibition of drug behaviour is misguided and wrong; as Herbert Packer, in his classic 1968 work, *The Limits of the Criminal Sanction*, wrote: 'A clearer case of misapplication of the criminal sanction would be difficult to imagine.'[176]

5. The Failure of Prohibition

This chapter assesses the practical consequences of drug policy. Such an assessment, as indicated at the beginning of the preceding chapter, is often portrayed as a purely 'technical' analysis. Consider, for example, the following assertion by Paul Taubman: 'Whether or not decriminalization of drugs is a sensible policy depends on the costs and benefits to society of such a policy.'[177] This criterion is established by Taubman in the context of a 'long intellectual history [in economics] concerning the appropriateness of the intervention of governments in an individual's determination of the allocation of resources and activities'.[178] Although this approach presents itself as purely technical – based on the measurement of costs and benefits – and therefore morally neutral, it is in fact neither of these. A cost-benefit analysis of drug policy typically considers issues such as the social costs of prohibition-related crime and law enforcement, and benefits such as the productivity and 'normal' health of those deterred from 'anti-productive' and 'harmful' drug use. It is committed, to some extent at least, to the moral value of economic efficiency. It presupposes, in other words, an *economic morality*. The application of economic theory to legal and policy analysis is a powerful trend in jurisprudence.[179] In its present form, it originates from a desire to set up a more sophisticated calculus than the Benthamite 'felicific calculus' – the vague Utilitarian target of the 'greatest good of the greatest number'. Whether one agrees with the approach or not, or whether one considers it a useful rather than an ultimate tool for analysis, it is certainly not correct to suggest that it should be rejected because it eschews 'values';[180] it simply creates its own value-system, its own moral calculus.

The broad terms of this technical value-system provide an opportunity to introduce some evidence in support of the claims that prohibition is ineffectual and irresponsible. I will consider each claim in turn. First, are present Irish drug controls effective? The short answer is no. As I have already indicated, the main strategies of the war on drugs – operating at both the domestic and international levels – are referred to as supply reduction and demand reduction. The former aims to reduce the availability of illicit drugs and the latter (which includes educative strategies) to deter people who might otherwise try these drugs. There is no question that, on both counts, the strategies are meeting with *some* success. It is, however, success of a very limited and deceptive kind.

Despite the attempts to reduce the supply of prohibited drugs, they continue to be available. In addition, it is agreed by most people involved in supply reduction that they are likely to remain available given the multiplicity of supply lines and the impossibility of closing all of them. The occasional drug seizures which are sensationalized by the media, in other words, are merely the tip of an iceberg. The drugs economy incorporates international and domestic networks of production and trafficking lines which leave no part of the globe untouched. Further, the three most well-known centres of illicit drug production – the 'cocaine triad' of Peru, Bolivia and Columbia, the 'golden crescent' of Pakistan and Afghanistan, and the 'golden triangle' at the borders of Burma, Thailand and Laos – all provide examples of economies that are heavily reliant on drug production. A 1989 Executive Survey of the United States Congressional Research Service noted that

> If law enforcement efforts are successful, without accompanying economic programs, the possible conse-quences include: massive increases in unemployment, major currency devaluations, collapse of entire regional economies, [and] a flood of new migrants to shanty towns in the cities. . . .[181]

Although this statement was made in the Latin American context, it has universal validity. Official discourse about drug problems and policies, however, rarely includes any discussion of the economic plight of many drug-producing countries. Neil Boyd and John Lowman have referred to evidence, in the context of the 'the geo-graphy of profit' in the global drug economy, of coca-producing farmers receiving 'one-fifth of 1 percent' of the money generated by their work, some of the remainder being siphoned off by local drug barons and corrupt politicians, with the bulk going to drug distributors in Europe and the United States.[182] Not surprisingly, the increase in lands devoted to illicit drug production has coincided with the rising International Monetary Fund debts in many of these countries; it is clear that 'until there are viable economic alternatives to coca, marijuana or poppy production, the war on drugs will not have much of an impact on production patterns'.[183]

Supply-side policies are also flawed in that the incentive to participate in the drug economy cannot be neutralized while profits remain as substantial as under present black market conditions: 'Wars against drugs fail because drugs and drug profits are more powerful motivators than drug laws. Drug dealers usually prevail because they are ruthless entrepreneurs fighting government bureaucrats who are paid whether they stop drug dealing or not.'[184] To give an example that reflects international statistics relating to virtually all illicit drugs, Superintendent John McGroarty, the former Garda Drugs National Liaison Officer, has written of interdiction efforts that 'cannabis seizures in Europe in 1993 amounted to £170 million, with law-enforcement agencies indicating via Interpol that a mere 10 per cent of the quantities available were seized'.[185]

Attempts at demand reduction have similarly failed. The consumption levels of many drugs continue at high levels and illicit drugs which have been introduced relatively recently into Ireland, such as Ecstasy, metaamphetamine, and crack, have found ready-made markets.[186] In May 1995, for example, it was estimated that somewhere in the region of 50,000 Ecstasy tablets are being sold every week in Ireland.[187] Preventive (as opposed to informative) drug education would appear to have had little impact on the willingness of Irish people to consume drugs. Indeed, international research consistently indicates that 'drug and alcohol education, even when it has not proved counterproductive, has failed to slow down or prevent initiation of alcohol consumption or illicit drug use by teenagers and young adults'.[188] Alluding to the ready availability of nicotine and alcohol products, Shane Butler has commented that the fundamental problem of current forms of alcohol and drug education is 'that preventive work of this kind cannot be entirely rational or characterised by logical consistency if national and international policies on these matters generally lack these characteristics'.[189]

Drugs therefore continue to be prohibited 'with varying degrees of severity and a high degree of inefficacy'.[190] It may well be argued in response that present efforts are the best that can be done, both in Ireland and elsewhere. The real problem, however, is that the war on drugs is not only a practical failure in terms of not meeting its objectives, it is also irresponsible in the sense that it generates enormous and unjustified social costs. These include: the costs of prohibition-related crime; the economic costs of drug-law enforcement, including policing, judicial system and incarceration costs; the tendency towards the encroachment of civil liberties which inevitably accompanies drug criminalization; and the alienation from the rule of law which many otherwise law-abiding citizens experience because of drug prohibition.

In most Western countries, the 'drugs problem' is perceived by many as part of the larger crime problem. Upon closer examination, much drug-related crime takes place not because of drug use or misuse but rather because drugs are criminalized, i.e. because of prohibition. Drug prohibition causes crime in two distinct ways. Firstly, it creates a black market which has the effect of artificially inflating drug prices, placing heavy financial burdens on regular drug users and thereby causing many to commit acquisitive crime. Thus, Paul O'Mahony, in *Crime and Punishment in Ireland*, notes that although 'the main category of drug offence form only a fraction of serious crime', his research showed that 'it was clear that a large majority of drug abusers were convicted for various crimes of theft rather than for drug offences as such'.[191] O'Mahony suggests that it is 'reasonable to assume from this and from the secretive, undercover nature of most illegal drug trading and use that the dark figure of crime in this area is very large'.[192] In the sense that prohibition has the effect of drawing many drug users into the criminal world, the deterrence approach can be seen as a self-fulfilling prophecy: it creates a legal and social atmosphere in which matters for the drug user will almost inevitably go from bad to worse.

Secondly, drug prohibition also contributes to levels of crime through the involvement of crime gangs in the trafficking of drugs. Again, it is not drugs, but rather drug prohibition, which creates this environment. The dramatic increase in the number of 'territorial' and other drug-related murders which have occurred in Dublin during this decade is a manifestation of this form of drug-related crime.[193] It is significant, particularly given this contemporary association of drugs with crime, that the *per capita* murder and assault-by-firearm rate rose steadily while alcohol prohibition was in effect in the United States and fell for ten straight years after that.[194] That particular prohibition was abandoned not only because of the flagrant disregard for the law on the part of millions of citizens but also because of the increased organization of crime that it engendered.

In terms of the direct economic costs of drug prohibition, the strain placed on our police resources, our court system, and our prison system is incalculable. This cost, including that which was directed to the failed 'fight against drugs' is, of course, borne ultimately by the taxpayer. It was estimated in 1991, for example, that the average cost of incarcerating a prisoner for one year was £36,000, about 3.5 times each Irish citizen's share of the national Gross Domestic Product.[195] Due to the fact that so much drug-related imprisonment is on the basis of convictions for theft and other 'non-drug' offences, it is difficult to estimate the precise costs involved. It is sufficient, however, to remark that the argument that these costs are not substantial has never been made by those who continue to advocate the 'drug war'. This economic cost can also be measured in terms of the opportunity costs of prohibition. These include those crimes which cannot be investigated properly because of the pursuit of drug offenders, the lack of financial resources which are made available to provide proper drug education and awareness programmes, and the delays experienced in our judicial system due to drug-related prosecutions.[196] It is worth drawing attention at this juncture to the particular notoriety which the prison situation in Ireland is gaining: the high incidence of drug misuse in Mountjoy Prison has recently been confirmed by an official government report.[197] As has been remarked of the situation in the United States: 'The evidence of the ultimate failure of drug war is the fact that even the tightly controlled atmosphere of a prison is rarely drug-free.'[198]

Another highly significant social cost of drug prohibition is the abuse of civil liberties which inevitably accompanies the active criminalization of basically 'victimless' conduct. It has been noted, for example, that the discussion in the *Government Strategy* concerning the detention of individuals suspected of concealing drugs in body cavities 'contains no reference to civil libertarian issues or to the general sensitivity of this issue'.[199] Further, the Irish Criminal Justice (Drug Trafficking) Act 1996 introduces seven-day detention for suspected drug dealers. This legislation was the subject of criticism from the Irish Council of Civil Liberties,[200] and its negative aspects were also highlighted in an article published in the Incorporated Law Society of Ireland's *Gazette*. The article describes the bill as 'a risk to the civil liberties of all citizens', and also notes: 'Solicitors believe, from practical experience, that such powers would be generally used against vulnerable drug addicts who have become the tools of major drug dealers rather than against the drug dealers themselves.'[201] The general tendency towards regarding increased police power as part of a panacea for the 'drug problem', in its failure to properly and consistently appreciate the context of drug use and drug misuse in Irish society (or, indeed, the difference between these two phenomena), has been characterized by Niall Stokes, editor of *Hot Press*, as a 'spurious consensus based on a combination of ignorance and prejudice'.[202]

Finally, the consequences for a legal system of attempting to uphold legislation which is unenforceable and which patently fails in its aims are difficult to quantify but certainly include an undermining of the authority of that legal system, a development that can have repercussions far beyond the narrow scope of any particular legislation. Insofar as the war on drugs includes, to cite the most obvious example, the 'criminalization' of cannabis, it amounts to crude and unwise abuse of state power. In the United States, the National Academy of Sciences 1982 report, *An Analysis of Marijuana Policy*, stated that 'Alienation from the rule of law in democratic society may be the most serious cost of current marijuana laws.'[203] Here, the 1991 *Government Strategy* indicates that over 70 per cent of persons charged with drug offences in 1990 were charged with cannabis-related offences.[204] Although some local police practices may not favour the prosecution of those found in possession of cannabis that is intended for personal use only,[205] the users still know that they are breaking the law when they possess or purchase the substance. This process of alienation is by no means limited to cannabis. Janet Paraskeya, director of the British National Youth Agency, has pointed out that the entire legal regime of drug prohibition

> criminalises large numbers of young people for whom drug use is problematic neither to themselves nor to society. Worse, it suggests to young people that society neither understands nor cares about their culture, thus making it difficult for youth workers to get down to the real business of drug education.[206]

These are the more significant practical social costs of an ineffective policy. No other aspect of social policy could possibly survive with such a record. The attitude on the part of public representatives that refuse to discuss this policy openly is unacceptable. The reality is that open debate could mean shifts, even if only temporarily, in the burden of proof. To prevail in a cost-benefit analysis, after all, as James Ostrowski has observed, prohibitionists must demonstrate that *all* of the following are plausible forecasts:

(1) Drug use would increase substantially after legalization; (2) The harm caused by any increased drug use
would not be offset by the increased safety of legal drug
use; (3) The harm caused by any increased use would
not be offset by a reduction in the use of dangerous
drugs that are already legal (such as alcohol and
tobacco); and (4) The harm caused by any increased
drug use not offset by items 2 or 3 would exceed the
harm now caused by the side effects of prohibition
(such as crime and corruption).[207]

In the meantime, despite the latent 'criminalization' of thousands of
young people, despite the incredible costs of the policy, and despite
its ineffectiveness (which can only benefit those who control the
illicit drug economy), the war on drugs continues unabated.

6. LEGALIZATION

The most important question regarding legalization, as was stated in
the introductory chapter of this pamphlet, is not whether criminal
law should play a role in this area, but rather how such a criminal
law should be constructed. Legalization, according to all of its
proponents in the international drug-policy debate, would include
restrictions and conditions on the distribution and sale of drugs, and
would also mean that those restrictions and conditions applied
differently to different drugs. Legalization is not proposed as the
'solution' to the problems associated with drugs. The discussions in
chapters 3 and 4 demonstrate that no specific drug policy measure
can even come close to attaining that goal. Indeed, as with problematic social phenomena of any kind, there is no 'solution' in the

true sense. However, the legalization of the psychoactive substances that are currently prohibited by law is a highly effective and available means of harm reduction.

The regulation and standardization of drugs and the development of informal social controls are among the more obvious benefits of legalization. Harm caused by drugs is far less likely to take place when drug policy is founded on regulation, informative education, and openness. Impure drugs and ignorance thrive where the illicit drug market is subjected to no controls or scrutiny whatsoever, and where official 'information' concerning the substances emphasizes only the dangers – an aspect of drugs that users know is only a partial account.

At the same time, any change in the law should certainly be undertaken gradually and with due care:

> In containing drug problems it is important to recog-
> nize that the criminal status of drug use is a major factor
> in causing problems for addicts and the community in
> general. However . . . the transition from the present
> situation to a more measured response to drugs should
> be a gentle one. It would seem unwise to make too
> many (new) drugs publicly available in a short time,
> because time is required for society to 'domesticate'
> new drugs for general usage and to adapt to a new way
> of thinking.[208]

Considerations of space make a detailed analysis of various systems of drug legalization impossible here. The brief discussion of legalization that follows will, however, raise the most significant aspects of this policy option.

A suitable starting-point is the progressive drug policy of the Netherlands. Dutch drug policy, although incorporating harm-reduction elements, is *not* one of 'legalization'. Its distinctive nature – a form of 'decriminalization' characterized by tolerance and expediency – is based on the distinction between soft drugs such as cannabis, and hard drugs such as cocaine and heroin.[209] Although the law is strictly observed as far as the manufacture of, or traffic in, illicit drugs is concerned (notably hard drugs), relatively little action is taken against possession of small quantities of any drugs for personal consumption. The distinction between hard and soft drugs is drawn primarily with a view to separating the market for cannabis from the market for other drugs; the sale of cannabis in 'coffee shops' is openly tolerated. The following passage from a 1994 Dutch drug policy statement captures the philosophy underlying the general policy approach:

> The central objective is to restrict as much as possible the risks that drug abuse presents to drug users them- selves, their immediate environment and society as a whole. These risks, or the likelihood of harmful effects, are dependent not only on the psychotropic or other properties of the substance, but primarily on the type of user, the reasons for use and the circumstances in which the drugs are taken. Experience has shown that a pragmatic approach aimed at seeking solutions for more concrete problems is more effective than one that is emotional and dogmatic. . . . Although the risks to society must of course be taken into account, the gov- ernment tries to ensure that drug users are not caused more harm by prosecution and imprisonment than by the use of the drugs themselves.[210]

In terms of the costs and effectiveness of the policy generally, Richard Stevenson notes that the Dutch government 'spends rela- tively far less than the UK government on law enforcement and more on services to drug users'.[211] He adds:

The decriminalisation of possession removes large numbers of offenders from the courts, and sparing use of prison sentences involves particularly high-cost savings. Drug-related crime is minimal and in general terms, the social and economic cost of drug abuse seems much lower in Holland than it is in the UK.[212]

However, the present trend of Dutch policy, as a result of pressure from the international community, is away from legalization and towards greater restrictions on the traffic in drugs.[213] One commentator has noted: 'As the result of this (enforced) change of course the problem will become less controllable and cause more criminalization and marginalization of the most vulnerable groups in [Dutch] society.'[214]

Criminalization and marginalization continue precisely because the Dutch model has not gone far enough. The major advantage of a scheme of legalization in which the *trade* in drugs is officially sanctioned and, as with other commerce, at least monitored by the state, is also noted by Stevenson. He remarks that all non-prohibition options short of legalization

. . . represent easements of policy as it applies to users rather than dealers. Decriminalisation is only a partial approach. It does not tackle the illegal trade which prospers from an increase in drug use and sponsors terrorism and political corruption. Legalisation deals directly with the fundamental problem which is to wrest control of drug markets from criminals.[215]

The way to win this aspect of the drug war is through the realization that prohibition, not drugs, causes drug-related crime; once this is realized fully, the drugs economy – the criminals' *raison d'être* – can be taken away from them.

The major objection to legalization relates to the elasticity of the demand for drugs, that is, the extent to which the quantity of drugs that a consumer purchases is affected by supply or price alterations. Anthony Lejeune, for example, writes: 'I still find the argument of the legalisers totally unpersuasive. . . . The point is that legalising drugs would really beyond doubt, increase their consumption: the only open questions are how large the increase would be and how many of the new drug-takers would ruin their lives.'[216] These comments are, of course, highly speculative; others have claimed that, on the contrary, 'citizens of the West do not customarily behave like an unthinking bovine herd, ready to ingest anything placed before them that is cheap and plentiful'.[217] On this difference of opinion, Ethan Nadelmann has commented as follows:

> the wide disparities are . . . primarily a reflection of visceral fears, beliefs and instincts regarding individual and collective human nature. . . . The roots of this . . . debate can be found in a related difference of opinions regarding the balance of power between psychoactive drugs and the human will. Prohibitionists typically see the balance favoring the former, with its potential to disrupt and destroy the lives of consumers. Legalizers, by contrast, emphasize the latter, with its assumption that the balance of basic human desires in most people effectively limits the destructive potential of drugs.[218]

The evidence is certainly not there to substantiate the danger of massive and sustained increases in use. Apart from the absence of any such developments in the Netherlands,[219] the American states that decriminalized marijuana possession in the 1970s not only generally reported savings in police and judicial resources but also maintained cannabis use rates close to the states retaining criminal sanctions.[220]

In terms of any automatic progression, via a 'gateway', from weaker to stronger drugs, the subsequent use or misuse of, for example, heroin, by former cannabis smokers, or, for that matter, alcohol consumers, has its roots in the same complex set of psychological, social, cultural and economic factors which underlie all drug use. As Jara Krivanek notes in a reference to classic empirical studies on this subject:

> . . . what the general public and some professionals often overlook is the fact that involvement with one drug does not *necessarily* mean progression to the next one. Virtually all marijuana users had earlier used alcohol or cigarettes, usually both; but only a percentage of alcohol and cigarette users [about 45 per cent], go on to use marijuana. A tiny fraction of these, some 3 per cent, then go on to try heroin.[221]

Again, the key is not exposure to the drugs in question, but rather the environmental determinants. To refer again to the 'transformation remedy' of socialist redistribution, drug 'progression' will only be altered, whether in a 'legalized' situation or under present circumstances, by channelling individual energies in more positive and productive directions than is possible under current forms of social and economic organization.

It is only possible to make some brief specific comments about the more well-known drugs. First, the case of cannabis. The 1991 *Government Strategy* acknowledges (in a rare reference to the use–misuse distinction in terms of an illicit drug) that while 'cannabis use seems to be on the increase among young people, it is usually not an ongoing regular pattern of misuse'.[222] In terms of the debate generally, there is no strong case for the criminal prohibition of this relatively innocuous drug. Cannabis, in standardized form, should be available for purchase to those over eighteen, with similar restrictions concerning time and place of sale as presently exist regarding alcohol. One writer has sensibly suggested that the 'use of legal marijuana would be accompanied by strong penalties for driving under its influence' and that 'the development of [alternative] delivery systems so that [cannabis] could be consumed by methods other than combustion, volatilization, and inhalation' should be encouraged.[223] It should also be noted here that a further argument for cannabis legalization is that the hemp plant (from which it derives) is one of the richest natural resources known to human-kind, capable of producing paper, linen, canvas, and fuel at highly conservational rates; 'it is . . . being claimed that the hemp plant could provide the western world with an ecological as well as an economic blessing'.[224]

As regards heroin, Niall Stokes has put forward a view that I have mentioned above in relation to the debate generally:

> It seems blindingly obvious to me that the best way to beat the drug barons is to take their market away from them. This can be done in two ways: by education and rehabilitation; and by supplying heroin – not metha-done – cheaply, to registered addicts. And if, to do this, it is necessary to legalise heroin and create a legitimate trade in the drug under State supervision, then that is the route to go.[225]

Although Fr Sean Cassin of the Merchant's Quay Drug Addict Support Group in Dublin and Paul O'Mahony, whose work on criminology has been referred to in this pamphlet, have both sup-ported Stokes' comments, other reactions were generally negative.[226] Stokes' suggestion is perfectly reasonable and needs to be con-sidered with due seriousness. As indicated by the discussion in the Appendix, the ingestion of heroin under circumstances such as those that would exist in a 'legalized' system would be far safer than under present circumstances. As another aspect of harm reduction in relation to heroin, the long established use of naxolene in emer-gency resuscitation of patients with opiate overdose suggests that its distribution to opiate misusers should be considered seriously for trial and evaluation.[227]

As for cocaine, John Kaplan's attitude is that consumption would increase if cocaine was easily available and inexpensive since 'the most important fact about cocaine is that it is an extremely attractive drug'.[228] E.J. Mishan, however, has a different view: 'Were the trade in cocaine to be decriminalised, it is reasonable to expect that, after some initial experimenting, the pattern would not be dissimilar to that of alcohol.'[229] The significant point here, as stated in the Appendix, is that most cocaine users do not become dependent on the drug and suffer no serious physical or social problems from it. On the basis of current knowledge, the same can be said about Ecstasy (MDMA). Meanwhile, the costs of the criminalization of cocaine and Ecstasy, in both local and global terms, are enormous. And, as with heroin, the danger of harmful effects from impure forms of these drugs is far greater when a policy of prohibition and denial is in force.

Hallucinogens were discussed publicly for the first time after the publication during the 1950s of Aldous Huxley's two essays, *The Doors of Perception*[230] and *Heaven and Hell*.[231] Huxley describes how mescaline enabled him to discover what he calls a 'sacramental vision of reality'. The 'inventor' of LSD, Albert Hofmann, has written: 'Wrong and inappropriate use has caused LSD to become my problem child . . . I see the true importance of LSD in the possibility of providing material aid to meditation aimed at the mystical experience of a deeper, comprehensive reality. Such a use accords entirely with the essence and working character of LSD as a sacred drug.'[232] As implied by the discussion in the Appendix, these drugs are certainly the ones that require the greatest educative effort. Their availability should perhaps be the most restrictive of all drugs under a 'legalized' regime. Again, however, criminal prohibition is completely unacceptable.

The distribution and control of drugs under any system of legalization is a subject that requires serious attention and planning. There may be a case – since private enterprise would appear particularly inappropriate – for the establishment of an innovative social service, specifically designed to monitor and regulate drug consumption in as safe a manner as acceptable and possible. Medical assistance and involvement in the distribution of certain drugs could be included, along with the co-operation of other social services. Preventive and informative educational efforts could also be incorporated, as well as responsibility for undertaking the research required to monitor the impact of normalization policies – *diachronic forms of longitudinal study*.[233]

7. CONCLUSION

Despite its inherent inconsistencies and contradictions, and despite the extent of social damage that it is causing rather than preventing, the war on drugs continues to be advocated by the majority of public representatives with a unique steadfastness. Indeed, it has been suggested that the underlying logic and motivation of the war on drugs can be understood as a modern example of the theory used to justify the Inquisition, the doctrine of righteous persecution:

> The modern drug inquisitor is another Augustine dressed in secular garb. Whereas Augustine sought to save the religious heretic from a literal hell, the modern inquisitor seeks to 'save' the social heretic (the drug consumer) from the metaphorical 'hell' of his 'addiction.' And just as Augustine's theory wreaked havoc in previous centuries – so the same theory, when secularized and applied to the 'war on drugs,' has created social turmoil and devastated hundreds of thousands of lives through imprisonment.[234]

In an attempt to understand this mentality – where societies 'know' that drug users must be treated against their will – Thomas Szasz recounts the ancient Greek practice of periodically sacrificing, in either a symbolic or actual sense, a citizen of the *polis*.[235] The ceremony usually involved a ritual exit from the city followed either by a purely symbolic 'exorcizing' or, as was more rarely the case, an actual killing. The person sacrificed – the scapegoat – was called the *pharmakos*, the etymological root of pharmacology and pharmacopoeia. The process leading to the 'destruction' of the scapegoat, according to Szasz, was 'the most important and most potent "therapeutic" intervention known to "primitive" man'.[236]

Szasz argues that the war on drugs represents an instance of human sacrifice, or scapegoating. He suggests that among contemporary *pharmakoi* are '. . . certain substances, . . . certain entrepreneurs, . . . and certain persons who use certain prohibited substances'.[237] Citing the work of Jane Ellen Harrison, and in particular her suggestion that a fundamental law of both social organization and religious ritual is 'the conservation and promotion of life',[238] Szasz writes:

> Individuals and societies thus seek to include that which they consider good, and to exclude that which they consider evil. This principle may also be inverted: individuals or groups may, and often do, promote or prohibit certain substances to justify defining them as good or bad. The ritual thus symbolizes and defines the character of the substance that is ceremonially sought or avoided, and the belief about the goodness or badness of the substance in turn supports the ritual. This explains the social stability of such beliefs and rituals and their relative immunity to 'rational' or 'scientific' arguments seeking to alter them. It also explains why some individuals and groups are as deeply committed to the (ritual) use of certain substances – such as alcohol

or opium, beef or pork – as others are to their (ritual) avoidance.[239]

There is a major difference, however, between the modern 'pharmacological scapegoat' and the Greek *pharmakos*. The latter was essentially an object in a purification ceremony. The contemporary version (when an individual rather than a drug),

> although still an expendable person, is both object and subject, thing and agent: he or she is an effigy or symbol – the scapegoat – in a purification ceremony; and also a participant – the addict or pusher – in a counterceremony celebrating a substance tabooed by society's dominant ethic.[240]

This 'participation' of contemporary *pharmakoi* constitutes 'enemy activity' in the war on drugs. The war is a ceremony of scapegoating through which 'Man, the god of chemistry, seeks to purify his polluted earthly Garden'.[241] 'Drugs', the basic *pharmakos*, are the 'origin of difference and division', representing 'evil both introjected and projected'.[242] Christopher Norris captures the 'differentiation' ideology underlying scapegoating succinctly: the *pharmakos* is 'a necessary evil that society tolerates only in the hope of preventing worse ills'.[243]

Crucially, however, there is no real 'differentiation'. Drugs are used by the vast majority of citizens, and illicit drug use cannot even be prevented in prisons. Moreover, the problems associated with drugs, when closely examined, only serve to highlight more serious 'ills' in contemporary society. These problems have much deeper roots than the effects of any chemical: the fixation with these effects and the 'moral standards' which their enjoyment are said to violate obscure not only the harmlessness of much illicit drug use, but also the complex of social, economic, cultural, and psychological factors which contribute to addictive and destructive behaviours of *all* kinds – those related to social organization generally as well as to drug misuse. So too does the frenzy with which prohibitionist laws are defended. The following comment by William Duncan in the context of other public policy debates in Ireland is also appropriate here:

> Like the moth who is allured and blinded by the flame, there is always the danger of forgetting, through the excitement and publicity which legal debate engenders, the other social and economic factors which influence conduct and values.[244]

There remains, however, the possibility of change. Although engendering crisis at one level, the New World Order and the questioning philosophical perspectives which coexist with it have clearly contributed to more thoughtful reflection and assessment of the domestic policies of many Western governments, and these forms of fresh analysis have not excluded the question of the role that drugs play in contemporary society. Although the numbers of those beginning to fully recognize and appreciate the scapegoating process in their midst may remain relatively small, I would suggest, in conclusion, that the slowly developing process of questioning present drug policies will continue, and that these questions will lead ultimately to rejection of the war on drugs. One advocate of drug legalization has pointed out that, at the time of the Wickersham Committee's 1931 report that alcohol prohibition in the United States was not working, repeal advocates 'estimated that it would take a generation to repeal Prohibition, but it took only another two years'.[245] The normalization perspective of current illicit drug use could well gain favour in a similarly surprising fashion. Any switch from denial to acknowledgement is a potentially painful one. The only analgesic which will be effective in these circumstances includes not only a true understanding of the complexity and ambiguity inherent in the normalization perspective on drug policy but also the activation of social policies motivated by socialist redistribution and deconstructive awareness.

This pamphlet has attempted to highlight that problematic drug use is symptomatic, not causal. The option of denying this simple truth is no longer available. It is now necessary for us, as a society, to develop the maturity that is required to replace hysteria and misinformed fear with serious-minded and rational responses to the challenges posed by drugs. The reduction of the harmful effects of drugs requires a system of legalization. If the *minimization* of those effects is desired, then that legalization must be accompanied by other social policies, directed towards the problems that the 'war on drugs' helps us to forget.

APPENDIX

Alcohol has been descibed as 'almost certainly the oldest mood-altering drug used by man'.[246] It is both a central nervous system depressant (a drug which decreases brain activity causing drowsiness or sleepiness and in some cases relief of anxiety) and a sedative. Its immediate effect is usually a reduction of anxiety, tension and inhibitions. Heavy drinking can lead to liver disease, coronary heart disease, high blood pressure, gastritis, peptic ulcers, and dementia.[247] Excessive use of alcohol is today linked to problems such as domestic violence and lost labour-hours, as well as to serious illness and death.

Tobacco, which comes from the dried leaves of the *nicotiana tabacum* plant, was introduced into Europe from America in the sixteenth century. Tobacco contains *nicotine*, a drug that was widely prescribed until the late eighteenth-century. Nicotine can act as both a central nervous system stimulant (a drug which can stimulate either bodily or mental activity, or both) and as a sedative, depending on the user's mood and personality. Long-term effects of nicotine can include angina, high blood pressure, peripheral vascular disease, stroke, peptic ulcers, and coronary thrombosis.[248] Tobacco causes approximately six thousand deaths each year in Ireland.[249]

There is evidence of the use of *cannabis* – or *marijuana* – during the Stone Age.[250] This substance is a product of the plant *Cannabis Sativa*, commonly denoted the hemp plant. It is usually smoked as either dried-leaf or resin. It can act as a central nervous system depressant or as a hallucinogen, depending again on the circumstances of use.[251] Preparations of the hemp plant have been in medical use for over two thousand years. Introduced into Western medicine in the mid-nineteenth century, these preparations were taken for a wide variety of complaints including anxiety, insomnia, rheumatic disorders, migraine, painful menstruation, strychnine poisoning and opiate withdrawal.[252] Judge Francis Young, a member of the American Drug Enforcement Administration, went so far as to say that it is possibly 'one of the safest therapeutically active substances known to man'.[253]

Opium has been in extensive use as a medicine and recreational drug for many thousands of years.[254] Obtained from the opium poppy (*papaver somniferum*), it is a brown, sticky substance. For most of its history, opium has been used in its raw state, but various derivatives and preparations were developed in Europe since the fifteenth century. *Morphine* is an alkaloid first derived from opium in 1803.[255] *Heroin*, a semi-synthetic derivative of morphine, was discovered in 1874. It was introduced into medical practice in 1898 when the Bayer Company of Germany sold it as a remedy for coughs. Today, it is sold in powder form and can be injected into the bloodstream or smoked. Long-term regular misuse of narcotic analgesics like heroin leads to constipation, reduced sexual drive, disruption of menstrual periods, and poor eating habits. On the other hand, Steven Duke and Albert Gross note that 'as with marijuana, study after study has failed to find that the regular use of heroin, in conditions of relatively free availability, produces any substantial adverse effects on mental or physical health'.[256] Again, as put by Edward Brecher, there is 'general agreement throughout the medical and psychiatric literature that the overall effects of opium, morphine, and heroin on the addict's mind and body under conditions of low price and ready availability are on the whole amazingly bland'.[257] The association of opiates with physical harm arises largely because of 'the manner in which the drugs are administered and the accompanying lifestyle. . . . [The] physical complications frequently found among addicts . . . are the result of unsterile injection practices, the sharing of syringes, the injection of drugs such as barbituates which are not designed to be injected, and also infection caused by contaminants found in illicitly manufactured heroin'.[258]

Leaves of the *coca* bush, which contain the anaesthetic and stimulant *cocaine*, have been chewed in the Andean regions of South America at least since the sixth century.[259] Cocaine itself was isolated in pure form in 1844 and soon became widely used;[260] the soft drink Coca-Cola, for example, contained cocaine until 1910.[261] On the long-term effects and risks of this drug, John Henry, in *The British Medical Association of Medicines and Drugs*, states that heavy, regular use can cause restlessness, anxiety, hyperexcitability, nausea, insomnia and weight loss, and that continued use may lead to increasing paranoia and psychosis.[262] Most cocaine users, however, do not become dependent on the drug and suffer no serious physical or social problems from it.[263] '*Crack*' is an extremely potent form of cocaine usually ingested in the form of crystals that are smoked.

Amphetamine (also referred to as '*speed*') is a central nervous system stimulant. Widely prescribed as an appetite suppressant in the 1950s and 1960s, regular use frequently leads to weight loss and constipation, and regular users may also become 'emotionally unstable'.[264] *MDMA* or '*Ecstasy*', also a central nervous system stimulant, was originally developed in 1914 as an appetite suppressant. Ecstasy is a 'designer drug', a drug produced by modifications to the structure of existing drugs (in this case, amphetamine). It is also popularly regarded as a 'dance drug' because of its strong association with youth dance culture. Prior to its criminalization in the United States, Ecstasy was used by several psychotherapists because of its renowned empathogenic qualities.[265] An article in a 1995 issue of the *Irish Pharmacy Journal* reported that frequent use can result in anorexia and weight loss, and that some users suffer from panic attacks and paranoia.[266]

LSD and *mescaline* are both hallucinogens. The ancient, well-integrated use of natural hallucinogenic drugs has been well documented.[267] The effects of usual doses of each drug lasts for between ten and twelve hours, and can include severe distortions in sound and vision, as well as increased introspection. LSD was accidentally discovered in 1943 by Dr Albert Hofmann at the Sandoz Company's pharmaceutical–chemical research laboratory in Switzerland. Mescaline originally derives from the peyote cactus but is now also available in synthetic form. These drugs, like MDMA, are presently regarded as having no legitimate medical uses although they have been used to treat patients by psychotherapists and psychiatrists.[268] The evidence is clear that considerations as to 'set' and 'setting' are crucial to the proper use of hallucinogens.[269] With all hallucinogens, there is a risk of unpleasant mental effects, particularly in those who are anxious or depressed. They may also increase the risk of mental disturbances, particularly in people with existing psychological problems.[270]

Other 'recreational' drugs include *vasidolators* (which increase the flow of blood by relaxing blood vessel walls giving the user a rapid rush of energy) such as *nitrites*. These drugs are very quick acting, their effects usually start within thirty seconds of inhalation and last for about five minutes. Lasting physical damage, including cardiac problems, can result from chronic use of these drugs.[271] Another group of drugs are the *volatile solvents*, such as glue and aerosols, which produce a mixture of sedative, anaesthetic and hallucinogenic effects. Due to the ready availability of solvents, young people with family and personality problems are particularly at risk of becoming habitual users.[272] Regular daily use of solvents can lead to pallor, fatigue and forgetfulness. Heavy use may affect school performance and lead to weight loss, depression and general deterioration of health.[273] *Benzodiazepines* are among the most commonly prescribed drugs. They are used mainly for short-term treatment of anxiety and stress and as sleeping drugs. Abuse is uncommon, but the typical misuser is a middle-aged or elderly person who may have been taking these drugs on prescription for months or years.[274] *Barbituates*, which are both depressants and sedatives, are similarly misused. In the past they were widely prescribed as sleeping drugs, but today they are mostly used in anaesthesia and for epilepsy.[275]

NOTES AND REFERENCES

1. Huxley, A., 'A treatise on drugs' [1931], in Horowitz, M. and Palmer, C. (eds.), *Moksha: Writings on Psychedelics and the Visionary Experience (1931–1963)* (New York: Stonehill, 1977), p. 5.

2. For a complete account of these perspectives, see Van de Wijngaart, G.F., *Competing Perspectives on Drug Use: The Dutch Experience* (Utrecht: Rijksuniversiteit te Utrecht, 1990), pp. 87–104.

3. *Government Strategy to Prevent Drug Misuse* (Dublin: Department of Health, 1991) [hereinafter *Government Strategy*].

4. For a discussion of the similarities and differences between pro- and anti-legalization advocates of harm reduction, see Nadelmann, E.A., 'Progressive legalizers, progressive prohibitionists and the reduction of drug-related harm', in Heather, N., Wodak, A., Nadelmann, E.A. and O'Hare, P. (eds.), *Psychoactive Drugs and Harm Reduction: From Faith to Science* (London: Whurr, 1993).

5. Intoxicating Liquor Act 1988.

6. Norrie, A., *Crime, Reason and History: A Critical Introduction to Criminal Law* (London: Weidenfeld and Nicolson, 1993), p. 27.

7. Corrigan, D., *Facts about Drug Abuse in Ireland*, 3rd edn. (Dublin: Health Promotion Unit, Department of Health, 1994), p. 2.

8. For further discussion of this legislation, see text *infra* at notes 65–70.

9. There are a number of ways in which histories of drug policy can be presented and interpreted. The bent of this paper, as the reader will be aware from the introductory section, is broadly critical. Critical work on the social history of deviance and social control has been concisely categorized into two types: 'critical psychiatry' and 'post-structuralist approaches' (see Ingleby, D., 'Professionals as socializers: The "Psy Complex"' (1985), 7, *Research in Law, Deviance and Social*

Control, pp. 79–109; see also discussion in Johnstone, G., 'From vice to disease? The Concepts of Dipsomania and Inebriety, 1860–1908' (1996) 5, *Social and Legal Studies*, p. 53 (note 3)). Whereas critical psychiatry has tended to place these processes in the broader context of Marxist historical analyses, poststructuralist approaches have drawn on the work of the French philosopher, Michel Foucault, and in particular his histories (or 'genealogies') of the asylum, the clinic, and the prison (*Madness and Civilisation* [1961] (New York: Pantheon, 1965); *The Birth of the Clinic: An Archaeology of Medical Perception* [1963] (London: Tavistock, 1973); *Discipline and Punish: The Birth of the Prison* [1975] (London: Penguin, 1991)). 'The purpose of history,' Foucault wrote, 'guided by genealogy, is not to discover the roots of our identity but to commit itself to its dissipation' ('Nietzsche, genealogy, history', in Bouchard, D.F. (ed.), *Language, Counter-Memory, Practice: Selected Essays and Interviews* (Ithaca: Cornell University Press, 1977), p. 162). Just as, for example, his genealogy of punishment (*Discipline and Punish*) sought to undermine the belief that prisons are an inevitable form of punishment, the discussion of historical drug-policy developments which follows here, while a far cry from being a 'genealogy', has a similar purpose in relation to the war on drugs.

10. Heather, N. and Robertson, I., *Problem Drinking: The New Approach* (London: Penguin, 1985), p. 21.

11. Ibid., p. 23.

12. Ibid., p. 32.

13. Ibid., p. 24.

14. Ibid., pp. 24–6.

15. Ibid., p. 25.

16. Gay, P., *The Cultivation of Hatred – The Bourgeois Experience: Victoria to Freud (Volume III)* (London: HarperCollins, 1994), p. 491.

17. Ibid., pp. 491–513.

18. Ibid., p. 509.

19. Heather and Robertson, op. cit., p. 121.

20. Ibid., p. 36.

21. Ibid., p. 31.

22. Stimson, G. and Oppenheimer, E., *Heroin Addiction: Treatment and Control in Britain* (London: Tavistock, 1982), p. 16.

23. Duster, T., *The Legislation of Morality: Law, Drugs, and Moral Judgment* (New York: The Free Press, 1970), p. 1.

24. Hayter, A., *Opium and the Romantic Imagination* (London: Faber and Faber, 1968), p. 34, quoted in Stimson and Oppenheimer, op. cit., p. 18.

25. Berridge, V., 'Morality and medical science: Concepts of Narcotic Addiction in Britain, 1820–1926' (1979) 36, *Annals of Science*, p. 70.

26. Rouse, J.J. and Johnson, B.D., 'Hidden paradigms of morality in debates about drugs: Historical and policy shifts in British and American drug policies', in Inciardi, J.A. (ed.), *The Drug Legalization Debate* (Newbury Park: SAGE, 1991), pp. 186–92.

27. Ibid., p. 190.

28. Stimson and Oppenheimer, op. cit., p. 21.

29. Ibid.

30. Ibid., pp. 21–2.

31. Ibid., p. 22. Interestingly, Stimson and Oppenheimer suggest that subsequent calls from the medical profession for stricter regulation of opiates were based primarily not on the problem of habituation but instead on 'the problem of working-class self-medication. . . . The position of the medical profession, expanding in size and moving out from treating a relatively affluent clientele, was threatened by working-class drug use, since drugs could be bought from pharmacists without prescription. . . . [Doctors] were aiming at a

monopoly on prescribing, and the [1868] Act did little to further this end' (ibid.).

32. Hamowy, R., 'Preventive medicine and the criminalization of sexual immorality in nineteenth century America', in Barnett, R.E. and Hagel, J. (eds.), *Assessing the Criminal: Restitution, Retribution, and the Legal Process* (New York: Ballinger, 1977), p. 44.

33. Berridge, op. cit., p. 77 (emphasis in original); for a discussion of the interrelation between medical and moral concerns in the separate inebriety movement, see Johnstone, op. cit.

34. Stimson and Oppenheimer, op. cit., p. 22.

35. See generally Musto, D.F., 'The history of legislative control over opium, cocaine, and their derivatives', in Hamowy, R. (ed.), *Dealing with Drugs: Consequences of Government Control* (Lexington: Lexington Books, 1987), p. 37; Duster, op. cit., pp. 3–28.

36. See Richards, D.A.J., 'Drug use and the rights of the person: A moral argument for decriminalization of certain forms of drug use' (1981), 33, *Rutgers Law Review*, pp. 632–5.

37. Hamowy, R., 'Introduction: Illicit drugs and government control', in Hamowy (ed.), op. cit., p. 12.

38. *Ex parte Yung Jon* 28 F. 308 (D. Ore. 1886), quoted in Bonnie, R.J. and Whitebread, C.H., 'The forbidden fruit and the tree of knowledge: An inquiry into the legal history of American marijuana prohibition' (1970), 56, *Virginia Law Review*, p. 997.

39. The American-inspired international drug-control movement had begun with the Shanghai Opium Commission in 1909. This led to the Hague Opium Convention of 1912, which placed the burden of drugs control on the domestic legislation of signatory states. It was agreed by each that the use of opium, morphine, and cocaine should be confined to medical purposes (see Musto, op. cit., pp. 47–51).

40. See generally Musto, op. cit., pp. 54–8.

41. Brecher, E. (and eds), *Consumer Reports: Licit and Illicit Drugs* (Boston: Little Brown and Company, 1972), p. 49.

42. 249 U.S. 96 (1919).

43. See generally Duster, op. cit., pp. 3–28.

44. Bonnie and Whitebread, op. cit., p. 990.

45. See Evans, K., 'Update on the US drug war', *New Law Journal* (16 February 1996), p. 207. Racial prejudice, particularly in relation to Mexican immigrants, also played a significant role in the prohibition of marijuana: see Bonnie and Whitebread, op. cit., pp. 1012–16.

46. Nixon, R., *Presidential Papers* (10 March 1969), cited in Slaughter, J.B., 'Marijuana history in the United States: History of a failed policy' (1988), 21, *Columbia Journal of Law and Social Problems*, p. 444 (note 134).

47. Britain had been a signatory to the 1912 Hague Convention (see note 39 *infra*). However, in line with the *Webb* decision in the United States, some domestic forces in Britain, including the Home Office, favoured stricter 'moral-legal' controls (Stimson and Oppenheimer, op. cit., pp. 23–6).

48. Departmental Committee on Morphine and Heroin Addiction, *Report* (London: HMSO, 1926), p. 11.

49. Ibid., p. 32.

50. Ibid.

51. Berridge, op. cit., pp. 84–5.

52. Stimson and Oppenheimer, op. cit., p. 31.

53. Ibid., p. 38.

54. Interdepartmental Committee on Drug Addiction, *Report* (London: HMSO, 1961), p. 9.

55. See Bean, P., *The Social Control of Drugs* (London: Martin Robertson, 1974), pp. 102–12.

56. Interdepartmental Committee on Drug Addiction, *Report* (London: HMSO, 1965), p. 8.

57. See generally Stimson and Oppenheimer, op. cit., pp. 49–54.

58. *Report* (1965), op. cit., p. 8.

59. Ibid., p. 6.

60. For further discussion of this system, see Bean, op. cit., pp. 79–83.

61. Turner, D., 'Pragmatic incoherence: The changing face of British drug policy', in Krauss, M.B. and Lazear, E.P. (eds.), *Searching for Alternatives: Drug-Control Policy in the United States* (Stanford: Hoover Institution Press, 1991), p. 179.

62. Downes, D., *Contrasts in Tolerance: Post-War Penal Policy in The Netherlands and England and Wales* (Oxford: Clarendon Press, 1988), pp. 126–7.

63. *Government Strategy*, p. 1.

64. *Report of the Working Party on Drug Abuse* (Dublin: Stationery Office, 1971).

65. Section 2.

66. Sections 3–4.

67. Section 5.

68. Sections 6–12.

69. Section 27.

70. Section 28.

71. Butler, S., 'Drug problems and drug policies: A quarter of a century reviewed' (1991), 39, *Administration*, p. 213.

72. Ibid., p. 231 (note 7).

73. Ibid., p. 215.

74. See O'Mahony, P., *Crime and Punishment in Ireland* (Dublin: Round Hall Press, 1993), pp. 66–8.

75. Dean, G., O'Hare, A., O'Connor, A., Kelly, M. and Kelly, G., 'The opiate epidemic in Dublin 1979–1983', *Irish Medical Journal* 78 (1985), pp. 107–10, cited in Butler, op. cit., pp. 218–19.

76. Butler, op. cit., p. 220.

77. 'Drug abuse and the Task Force' – press release issued by the Government Information Services on behalf of the Department of Health, 22 September 1983, quoted in Butler, op. cit., p. 220.

78. Sections 6–7.

79. Section 8.

80. Butler, op. cit., p. 223.

81. Ibid., p. 225.

82. *Government Strategy*, p. 23.

83. Butler, op. cit., p. 229.

84. Ibid., p. 230.

85. Criminal Justice (Miscellaneous Provisions) Bill 1996; Proceeds of Crime Bill 1996; Criminal Assets Bureau Bill 1996; Disclosure of Certain Information for Taxation and Other Purposes Bill 1996.

86. Miller, R., *The Case for Legalising Drugs* (New York: Praeger, 1991), p. 25.

87. Zinberg, N., *Drug, Set, and Setting: The Basis for Controlled Intoxicant Use* (New Haven: Yale University Press, 1984).

88. Ibid., p. 5.

89. Ibid., p. 172.

90. Ibid., pp. 172–3.

91. Ibid., p. 5.

92. Ibid., p. 5.

93. Ibid., p. 203.

94. Ibid., p. 203.

95. Richards, op. cit., pp. 650–1.

96. Krivanek, J., *Drug Problems, People Problems: Causes, Treatment and Prevention* (Sydney: Allen and Unwin, 1982), p. 91.

97. *Government Strategy*, p. 4.

98. Krivanek, J., *Addictions* (Sydney: Allen and Unwin, 1988), p. 32.

99. Ibid., p. 31. Krivanek notes that '. . . multifactorial etiologies are rapidly becoming the rule rather than the exception' (ibid.).

100. Willis, J.H.P., 'Drug addiction', in Duncan, R. and Weston-Smith, M. (eds.), *The Encyclopedia of Ignorance* (New York: Wallaby, 1978), p. 370, quoted in Marks, R., 'A freer market for heroin in Australia: Alternatives to subsidizing organised crime' (1990) *The Journal of Drug Issues*, 20 (1), p. 131.

101. 'Nomenclature and classification of drug and alcohol-related problems: A WHO Memorandum', (1981) *Bulletin of the World Health Organisation*, quoted in Krivanek, *Addictions*, p. 52.

102. Krivanek, *Addictions*, p. 52.

103. See e.g. O'Donnell, J.A., Voss, H.L., Clayton, R.R., Slatin, G.T. and Room, R.G.W., *Young Men and Drugs – A Nationwide Survey* (Rockville, Md.: National Institute on Drug Abuse, 1976), cited in Krivanek, *Addictions*, p. 34.

104. Ibid.; see also Zinberg, op. cit., pp. 12–15.

105. Krivanek, *Addictions*, p. 34.

106. Peele, S., 'A moral vision of addiction: How people's values determine whether they become and remain addicts' (1987) *The Journal of Drug Issues*, 17 (2), p. 202.

NOTES AND REFERENCES

107. Fox, R. and Mathews, I., *Drugs Policy: Fact, Fiction and the Future* (Sydney: The Federation Press, 1992), p. 11.

108. Krivanek, *Addictions*, p. 6.

109. Krivanek, *Drug Problems*, p. 79.

110. Miller, op. cit., p. 43.

111. Henry, J., (ed.), *The British Medical Association Guide to Medicine and Drugs*, 2nd edn. (London: Dorling Kindersley, 1991), p. 419.

112. Kendell, R.E., 'Alcoholism: a medical or political problem?', (1979), 1, *British Medical Journal*, p. 367.

113. See generally Heather and Robertson, op. cit., pp. 141–263.

114. Cahalan, D., *Problem Drinkers: A National Survey* (San Francisco: Jossey-Bass, 1970), quoted in Heather and Robertson, op. cit., p. 13.

115. See Heather and Robertson, op. cit., pp. 158–224.

116. See Morgan, M. and Grube, J.W., 'The Irish and alcohol: A classic case of ambivalence', *The Irish Journal of Psychology*, (1994), 15 (2 and 3), pp. 390–403.

117. Waters, J., 'Why drugs campaign is doomed to failure', *The Irish Times*, 1 August 1995.

118. Ibid.

119. Keenan, E., Gervin, M., Dorman, A. and O'Connor, J.J., 'Psychosis and recreational use of MDMA ("Ecstasy")' (1993) 10(3), *Irish Journal of Psychological Medicine*, pp. 162–3.

120. Zinberg, op. cit., p. 17. Zinberg comments: 'Without doubt the most important source of precepts and practices for control is the peer using group' (ibid., p. 18).

121. Zinberg, 'The use and misuse of intoxicants: Factors in the development of controlled use', in Hamowy (ed.), op. cit., p. 266.

81

122. See e.g. Marcenko, M.O. and Spence, M., 'Social and psychological correlates of substance abuse among pregnant women' (1995), 19 (2), *Social Work Research*, p. 103.

123. Krivanek, *Addictions*, p. 47.

124. Ibid.

125. O'Higgins, K. and O'Brien, M., *Treated Drug Misuse in the Greater Dublin Area: Report for 1994* (Dublin: The Health Research Board, 1995), p. 77.

126. Mc Cullagh, C., *Crime in Ireland: A Sociological Introduction* (Cork: Cork University Press, 1996), p. 221.

127. Kökény, M., Ajkay, Z., and Bognár, I., 'Risk factors investigation of health behaviour: Hungarian experiences', in Anderson, R., Davies, J.K., Kickbusch, I., McQueen, D.V. and Turner, J. (eds.), *Health Behaviour Research and Health Promotion* (Oxford: Oxford University Press, 1988), p. 77.

128. Anglin, M.D. and Hser, Y-I., 'Treatment of drug abuse', in Tonry, M. and Wilson, J.Q. (eds.), *Drugs and Crime (Crime and Justice: A Review of Research – Volume 13)* (Chicago: University of Chicago Press, 1990), p. 402.

129. Such treatment facilities are available in Ireland. For an account of services available in Dublin, see Brennan, P., 'Drugs: Where to go for help', *Hot Press*, 7 August 1996.

130. Kökeny, Ajkay, and Bognár, op. cit., p. 77.

131. See e.g. Szasz, T., 'The morality of drug controls' in Hamowy (ed.), op. cit., p. 346; Ostrowski, J., 'The moral and practical case for drug legalization' (1990), 18, *Hofstra Law Review*, p. 607.

132. Ginsberg, M., *On Justice in Society* (London: Harmondsworth, 1965), p. 236, cited in Daly, C., *Law and Morals* (Dublin: Four Courts Press, 1993), p. 33.

133. See Daly, op. cit., pp. 33–4.

134. Michaels, R.J., 'The market for heroin before and after legalization', in Hamowy (ed.), op. cit., p. 325.

135. See Mill, J.S., 'On Liberty' [1859], in *On Liberty and Other Essays* (Oxford: Oxford University Press, 1991), p. 5.

136. See Friedman, M., 'The war we are losing', in Krauss and Lazear (eds.), op. cit., p. 54.

137. See Stephen, J.F., *Liberty, Equality and Fraternity* [1873] (Cambridge, Mass.: Cambridge University Press, 1967).

138. See Smith, J.C. and Hogan, B., *Criminal Law*, 7th edn. (London: Butterworths, 1992), pp. 16–18.

139. Ibid., pp. 17–18.

140. Zimring, F.E. and Hawkins, G., 'The wrong question: Critical notes on the decriminalization debate', in Krauss and Lazear (eds.), op. cit., p. 26.

141. Binchy, W., 'Pluralism, liberty and the right to life', in Whelan, A. (ed.), *Law and Liberty in Ireland* (Dublin: Oak Tree Press, 1993), p. 138.

142. Johnstone, op. cit., p. 52.

143. Boyd, N. and Lowman, J., 'The Politics of Prostitution and Drug Control', in Stenson and Cowell (eds.), *The Politics of Crime Control* (London: SAGE, 1991), p. 123.

144. Fraser, N., 'From Redistribution to Recognition? Dilemmas of Justice in a "Post-Socialist" Age' (1995) 212, *New Left Review* pp. 78–82 (emphasis in original). Fraser argues, for example, that gender and 'race' are bivalent modes of collectivity. In both cases, there is a collectivity (women; people of colour) that is disadvantged in political-economic *and* cultural-valuational terms. These two aspects are not separate; instead, they intertwine to reinforce one another dialectically. Thus, women and people of colour are discriminated against because of sexist/ androcentric and racist/Eurocentric norms respectively. These norms are institutionalized in the state

and the economy. The economic disadvantage experienced by these collectivities restricts, in turn, the proper emergence of a collective 'voice' on the part of the groups, impeding equal participation in the making of culture, in public spheres, and in everyday life (ibid., pp. 78–82).

145. Ibid., pp. 82–86.

146. Davies, M., *Asking the Law Question* (Sydney: Law Book Company, 1994), p. 260. See e.g. Derrida, J., 'Force of law: The "Mystical Foundation of Authority"' (1990) 11, *Cardozo Law Review*, p. 919; Balkin, J.M., 'Deconstructive Practice and Legal Theory' (1987), 96, *Yale Law Journal*, p. 743; Devlin, R.F., 'Law, postmodernism and resistance: Rethinking the significance of the Irish hunger strike' (1994), 14, *Windsor Yearbook of Access to Justice*, p. 3.

147. Davies, op. cit., p. 254.

148. Balkin, op. cit., pp. 761–3. *Différance*, a key concept in deconstruction, is an 'invention' of Derrida: it combines the sense of deference or postponement with difference or non-identification. In terms of the identification of oppositional hierarchies ('visions' and 'countervisions') that is the basis for the deconstructionist approach, *différance* suggests mutual dependency and highlights the antinominal. See Derrida 'Différance' in *Margins of Philosophy* (Chicago: University of Chicago Press, 1982), p. 3

149. Devlin, op. cit., p. 22.

150. Fraser, op. cit., p. 83 (emphasis in original).

151. Klerman, G.L., 'Psychotropic hedonism vs. Pharmacological calvinism' (1972), 2, *Hastings Center Report*, pp. 1–3.

152. Kramer, P., *Listening to Prozac: A Psychiatrist Explores Antidepressant Drugs and the Remaking of the Self* (London: Fourth Estate, 1994), p. 274.

153. Blum, R., *Society and Drugs – Drugs I: Social and Cultural Observations* (San Francisco: Jossey-Bass, 1969), pp. 332–3, quoted in Miller, op. cit., p. 127.

154. Kramer, op. cit., pp. 263–4.

155. Ibid., p. 264.

156. Ibid.

157. Ibid., pp. 264–5.

158. Drennan, J., 'Exploding the "safe drugs" myth', *Sunday Independent*, 12 November 1995.

159. Mugford, S., 'Drug legalization and the "Goldilocks" problem: Thinking about costs and control of drugs', in Krauss and Lazear (eds.), op. cit., p. 39.

160. Ibid.

161. Ibid.

162. Kaplan, J., *The Hardest Drug: Heroin and Public Policy* (Chicago: University of Chicago Press, 1983), p. 238.

163. Mailer, N., 'The Playwright as Critic', in *The Essential Norman Mailer* (London: New English Library, 1983), p. 348.

164. See Kaplan, op. cit., p. 42.

165. Crofton, J. and Doll, R., 'Preface' (1996), 52 (1), *British Medical Bulletin (Tobacco and Health)*, p. 1.

166. Wilson, 'Against the Legalization of Drugs' (1990), 89 *Commentary*, p. 26.

167. Ibid.

168. Wilson, J.Q., 'Drugs and Crime', in Tonry and Wilson (eds.), op. cit., p. 523.

169. Duke, S.B., and Gross, A.C., *America's Longest War: Rethinking Our Tragic Crusade Against Drugs* (New York: G.P. Putman's Sons, 1993), p. 69.

170. Mc Cullagh, op. cit., p. 221.

171. Lyng, S., 'Edgework: A Social Psychological Analysis of Voluntary Risk-Taking' 1990, 95 (4), *American Journal of Sociology*, pp. 851–6.

172. Ibid., p. 882.

173. Zinberg, N., 'The Study of Consciousness States', in Zinberg, (ed.), *Alternate States of Consciousness* (New York: Free Press, 1977), p. 3.

174. Ibid.

175. Krivanek, *Addictions*, p. 28.

176. Packer, H., *The Limits of the Criminal Sanction* (Stanford: Stanford University Press, 1968), p. 333.

177. Taubman, P., 'Externalities and Decriminalization of Drugs', in Krauss and Lazear (eds.), op. cit., p. 91.

178. Ibid., p. 90.

179. See e.g. Posner, R., *Economic Analysis of Law*, 3rd edn. (Boston: Little Brown, 1988).

180. For this argument, see Fiss, O., 'The Death of the Law?' (1986), 72, *Cornell Law Review*, p. 1.

181. Cited in Fox and Mathews, op. cit., p. 115.

182. Boyd and Lowman, op. cit., pp. 122–3.

183. Ibid., p. 123.

184. Ostrowski, 'Moral and Practical Case', p. 608.

185. McGroarty, J., 'The Cannabis Debate: Looking for new answers where the law has failed', *The Irish Times*, 23 June 1994.

186. See Clark, S., 'Generation Ecstasy', *Hot Press*, 31 May 1995; Tyaransen, O., 'Into the West', *Hot Press*, 31 May 1995; Clark, 'Life in the Faster Lane', *Hot Press*, 29 January 1996; Walsh, L., and Woulfe, N., '"Crack" seizures ominous says drugs unit head', *The Sunday Tribune*, 18 February 1996.

187. Clark, 'Generation Ecstasy'.

188. Butler, S., 'Alcohol and Drug Education in Ireland: Aims, Methods and Difficulties' (1994) *Oideas*, Samhradh, p. 137.

189. Ibid.

190. Hobsbawm, E., *Age of Extremes – The Short Twentieth Century: 1914–1991* (London: Michael Joseph, 1994), p. 334.

191. O'Mahony, op. cit., pp. 66–7.

192. Ibid., p. 67.

193. See Holland, M., 'Fear Behind the Anger', *The Observer*, 30 June 1996.

194. Boaz, D., 'The Failure of Prohibition', *Economic Affairs*, February 1991, p. 12.

195. O'Mahony, op. cit., p. 98.

196. For an account of these delays generally, see Opinion, 'Our Courts in Crisis', *The Bar Review*, June 1996, p. 4.

197. For the discussion of drug problems in the prison, see Mountjoy Prison Visiting Committee, *Annual Report 1995* (Dublin: Department of Justice, 1996), pp. 41–4.

198. Zeese, K.B., 'Drug War Forever?', in Krauss and Lazear (eds.), op. cit., p. 251.

199. Butler, *Drug Problems and Policies in Ireland*, p. 229.

200. See Farrell, M., *I.C.C.L. Briefing Paper No. 2* (May 1996).

201. 'Viewpoint', *Law Society of Ireland Gazette* 90, March 1996, p. 53.

202. Stokes, N., 'The Message', *Hot Press*, 9 August 1995.

203. Cited in Slaughter, op. cit., p. 435.

204. *Government Strategy*, p. 8.

205. For discussion of this practice, see Tyransen and Clark, 'The New Deal', *Hot Press*, 15 November 1995 (interview with Superintendent John McGroarty).

206. Quoted in Campbell, D., 'Drugs – Legal and Illegal', *Prospect*, April 1996.

207. Ostrowski, 'Answering the Critics of Drug Legalization', in Krauss and Lazear (eds.), op. cit., p. 297.

208. Van de Wijingaart, op. cit., p. 118.

209. See generally van Kalmthout, A.M., 'Characteristics of Drug Policy in the Netherlands', in Albrecht and van Kalmthout (eds.), *Drug Policy in Western Europe* (Max Planck Institute, 1989), p. 262.

210. *Drug Policy in the Netherlands* (Rijswijk, 1994), The Netherlands Ministry for Welfare, Health and Cultural Affairs.

211. Stevenson, R., *Winning the War on Drugs: To Legalise or Not?* (London: Institute of Economic Affairs, 1994), p. 47.

212. Ibid.

213. See *Drugs Policy in the Netherlands: Continuity and Change* (Rijswijk, 1995). This document was prepared by the Dutch Ministry of Foreign Affairs, Ministry of Health, Welfare and Sport, Ministry of Justice, and Ministry of the Interior.

214. van Kalmthout, op. cit., p. 278.

215. Stevenson, op. cit.

216. Lejeune, A., 'Say no to decriminalisation!', *Economic Affairs*, February 1991, p. 19.

217. Mishan, E.J., 'Narcotics: The Problem and the Solution' (1990), 61, *Political Quarterly*, p. 443.

218. Nadelmann, op. cit., pp. 41–2.

219. See Dutch drug policy document, 1995, op. cit., pp. 8–11.

220. Slaughter, op. cit., p. 426.

221. *Drug Problems*, p. 8 (emphasis in original).

222. *Government Strategy*, p. 8.

223. Morgan, J.P., 'Prohibition is Perverse Policy: What was True in 1933 is True Now', in Krauss and Lazear (eds.), op. cit., pp. 417–21.

224. Evans, K., op. cit., p. 207. The hemp plant is currently being grown in County Carlow, on an experimental basis and under government licence, by Teagaisc.

225. Stokes, N., 'The Message', Hot Press, 29 May 1996. This editorial was written in the aftermath of the suicide of heroin addict, Carole Anne Daly, in a Dublin prison cell.

226. See Hot Press, 'Smack City', 12 June 1996. Fr Cassin noted that the vigilante killing in May 1996 of a heroin addict who was suffering from AIDS, Josie Dwyer, was in part attributable to the 'emotive, knee-jerk response which is based on a prohibitionist approach of "Drugs Out"'.

227. See Strang, J., Darke, S., Hall, W., Farrell, M., and Ali, R., 'Heroin overdose: the case for take-home naxolene', British Medical Journal, 8 June 1996, 312, 1435.

228. Kaplan, 'Taking drugs seriously' (1992), The Public Interest, pp. 40–1.

229. Mishan, op. cit., p. 443.

230. Huxley, The Doors of Perception [1954] (London: Panther Books, 1977).

231. Huxley, Heaven and Hell [1956] (London: Panther Books, 1977).

232. Hofmann, A., LSD: My Problem Child (New York: McGraw Hill, 1980), pp. xii, 209.

233. Van de Wijngaart, op. cit., p. 79. It is important to be aware that any of the possible forms that legalisation could take, insofar as the state would remain involved, might constitute an extension of social control, in the form of processes of 'inscription' or otherwise (see discussion in Mugford, S., 'Harm Reduction: Does it lead where its proponents imagine?', in Heather, Wodak, Nadelmann, and O'Hare

(eds.), op. cit., pp. 29–31). There is a related point: while Peter Kramer suggests that the 'pharmacological calvinism' of the United States is a bulwark against the possibility of any drug being used by the state to, for example, placate unrest or suppress resistance (Kramer, op. cit., pp. 272–5), his argument is not conclusive. As Jara Krivanek points out, drugs and coercion are already entwined: 'Since infancy today's children have been taught to open their mouths and swallow whatever was popped in to cure what ailed them and they have watched their parents do the same' (Krivanek, *Drug Problems, People Problems*, p. 73). Some would argue that drugs such as alcohol, heroin, and Ecstasy play a quasi-'soma' role already. Detailed discussion of these matters is beyond the scope of this pamphlet; at any rate, there is no aspect of these arguments, in the light of the other issues which are involved, that provides a strong argument for the retention of the present blanket criminal prohibition of drugs.

234. Smith, G.H., *Atheism, Ayn Rand, and Other Heresies* (1991) 233–4, quoted in Barnett, op. cit., p. 2613.

235. See Szasz, T., *Ceremonial Chemistry: The Ritual Persecution of Drugs, Addicts, and Pushers* (New York: Doubleday, 1974), pp. 19–27.

236. Ibid., p. 19.

237. Ibid., p. 20.

238. Harrison, J.E., *Epilegomena to the Study of Greek Religion and Themis: A Study of the Social Origins of Greek Religion* [1912, 1921] (New York: University Books, 1962), xvii, cited in Szasz, *Ceremonial Chemistry*, p. 23.

239. Szasz, *Ceremonial Chemistry*, p. 23.

240. Ibid., p. 26.

241. Ibid., p. 27.

242. Derrida, *Dissemination* (Chicago: University of Chicago Press, 1982), p. 133.

243. Norris, C., *Derrida* (London: Fontana, 1987), p. 42.

244. Duncan, W., 'Abortion, Divorce and the Debate about Liberty', in Whelan, (ed.), op. cit., p. 130.

245. Boaz, op. cit., p. 14.

246. Corrigan, op. cit., p. 19.

247. Henry (ed.), op. cit., p. 419.

248. Ibid., p. 424.

249. Health Promotion Unit, Department of Health, *Information on Smoking* (Dublin, 1993), p. 2.

250. Corrigan, op. cit., p. 29.

251. Henry (ed.), op. cit., p. 422.

252. Ibid., p. 422.

253. Quoted in Nadelmann, E. and Wenner, J., 'Toward a Sane National Drug Policy', *Rolling Stone*, 5 May 1994.

254. Stimson and Oppenheimer, op. cit., p. 13.

255. Ibid.

256. Duke and Gross, op. cit.,p. 62.

257. Brecher (et al), op. cit., p. 26.

258. Stimson and Oppenheimer, op. cit., p. 4.

259. Corrigan, op. cit., p. 47.

260. Szasz, *Ceremonial Chemistry*, p. 190.

261. Corrigan, op. cit., p. 47.

262. Henry (ed.), op. cit., p. 421.

263. Duke and Gross, op. cit., pp. 70–1; see also Kaplan, 'Taking Drugs Seriously', op. cit., p. 41.

264. Henry (ed.), op. cit., p. 420.

265. See Rosenbaum, M., and Doblin, R., 'Why MDMA Should Not Have Been Made Illegal', in Inciardi (ed.), op. cit., p. 135.

266. Corrigan, 'Ecstasy – A Fact File', *Irish Pharmacy Journal*, December 1995, p. 381.

267. See e.g. Furst, P.T., '"High States" in Culture-Historical Perspective', in Zinberg (ed.), *Alternate States of Consciousness*, op. cit., pp. 53–69.

268. See e.g. Grof, S., *LSD Psychotherapy* (Pomona: Hunter House, 1981).

269. Leary, T., Metzner, R. and Alpert, R., 'Psychedelic Sessions', in Miller, J. and Koral, R. (eds.), *White Rabbit: A Psychedelic Reader* (San Francisco: Chronicle Books, 1995), p. 129.

270. Henry (ed.), op. cit., p. 422.

271. Ibid., p. 424.

272. Ibid., p. 425.

273. Ibid.

274. Ibid., p. 421.

275. Ibid., p. 420.

6813